ADVANCE PRAISE FOR *Restoring the Teenage Soul*

"What Meg Meeker has accomplished with *Restoring the Teenage Soul* makes this the right book for these troubled times. If parents are looking for a place to better understand the pressure their teens are under today, *Restoring the Teenage Soul* is that resource."
— Melissa Cox, Managing Editor
The Complete Book of Baby and Child Care

"Looking for someone to hold up a mirror to the world that your teen lives in? Then Meg Meeker is that person, and her insights will amaze you. *Restoring the Teenage Soul* is a book every parent needs to read."
— Vickie Pangborn, L.P.N.
Mother of three

"When it comes to finding our way as parents of teens, I'm especially thankful I know an expert like Meg Meeker. If you're serious about understanding your teen's emotional, spiritual and physical needs — look no further than the pages of *Restoring the Teenage Soul.*
— Michael A. Jones, M.D., Chief,
Department of Pathology, Maine Medical Center

Restoring the Teenage Soul

Nurturing Sound Hearts and Minds in a Confused Culture

Margaret J. Meeker, M.D.

McKinley & Mann
Traverse City, Michigan

Published by MCKINLEY & MANN
940 Pine Ridge Dr.
Traverse City, Michigan 49686

Publisher's Cataloging-in-Publication Data
Meeker, Margaret J., M.D.
    Restoring the teenage soul: nurturing sound hearts and minds in a confused
    culture / Margaret J. Meeker, M.D. – Traverse City, Mich.: McKinley & Mann,
    1999.
        p.   cm.
    Includes bibliographical references.
    ISBN 0-9669894-0-6
        1. Teenagers.   2. Parent and teenager.   3. Adolescent psychology.
        I. Title.
HQ796 .M44   1999   99-60355
305.235   dc—21   CIP

PROJECT COORDINATION BY JENKINS GROUP, INC.

03 02 01 00 ◆ 5 4 3 2 1

Printed in the United States of America

To
Mother and Dad,
for all the right decisions they made.

CONTENTS

Foreword ix

Acknowledgments xi

Chapter One
JESSICA'S STORY 1

Chapter Two
ALLISON'S STORY 7

Chapter Three
MICHAEL'S STORY 13

Chapter Four
WHAT DO TEENS NEED? 19

Chapter Five
LOVE: GIVING AND RECEIVING 33

Chapter Six
VALUE OF THE SELF 41

Chapter Seven
SAFETY: PHYSICAL AND EMOTIONAL 51

Chapter Eight
TENDER HEARTS IN A TOUGH CULTURE 61

Chapter Nine
THE SEXUAL REVOLUTION: ITS EFFECT
ON PARENTS AND THEIR TEENS 69

Chapter Ten
THREE TOXIC MESSAGES   77

Chapter Eleven
BROKEN BODIES   85

Chapter Twelve
SHE WASN'T WELL AT ALL   97

Chapter Thirteen
BROKEN HEARTS   109

Chapter Fourteen
LOSS OF DEPENDENCE   119

Chapter Fifteen
A HOPE OF CONTROL   133

Chapter Sixteen
HOPE FOR PARENTS IS HOPE FOR TEENS   141

Chapter Seventeen
WHAT WE BELIEVE MATTERS   151

Chapter Eighteen
HELP FOR PARENTS EQUALS HELP FOR TEENS   159

Chapter Nineteen
MEETING THE LOVE NEEDS   169

Chapter Twenty
WAGING WAR   179

Endnotes   189
Bibliography   193
About the Author   197
Order Information   199

FOREWORD

by Elayne Bennett
Founder of Best Friends

ADOLESCENCE IS A TIME OF CONFLICT AND CONFUSION FOR MOST young people. Teen friendships and love relationships are transitory; there is pressure to achieve, to "fit in," to be popular and attractive. Many adolescents do not hold themselves in high regard, and the absence of self-worth can be a serious handicap, which makes them more vulnerable to negative peer pressure, early sexual activity, drug and alcohol abuse, and violent and aggressive behavior. As parents and concerned citizens we are appalled and confused at the tragic violent outbursts in our schools around the country. We cannot ignore these cries for help. If we do, we are "selling out" our future.

That is why *Restoring the Teenage Soul* should become a valuable resource for parents and professionals. Dr. Meg Meeker, a physician practicing child and adolescent medicine in Michigan, believes that parents need to see what she sees in her examination rooms: confused adolescents with emotional and health problems caused by lack of self-respect, depression, illegal drug and alcohol use, and sexual activity.

Not all teens are caught up in these behaviors but they are experiencing their glamorization in the media and pressure from their peers to join the "Just Do It" crowd. A critical mass of adolescent destructive behavior is threatening the future and the stability of our country. After all, we are talking about the next generation. We need our youth to mature and form strong marriages and families, so necessary for a moral and sound society.

ix

This why in 1987, I began to develop an educational curriculum for adolescent girls called Best Friends. As a faculty member of the Georgetown University Child Development Center, I had observed that little was being done in the area of adolescent development, especially to help girls cope with the pressures of early sexual intimacy. Girls at this age need and want friendship, to be part of a group, to discuss their personal concerns and receive support from friends and respected adults. I believed that girls could benefit from a sound program that promotes self-respect through self-restraint.

With help from friends and colleagues, I developed the Best Friends youth development program and implemented pilot programs in public schools in and around Washington D.C. My husband, Bill Bennett, former U.S. Secretary of Education and author of *The Book of Virtues,* has been one of our strongest supporters. Alma and Colin Powell, outstanding role models, provided vital encouragement to the growth of the program.

When Best Friends becomes part of a school curriculum (as it has in more than 79 schools in 14 states), we see dramatic results. A 1995 independent study of District of Columbia girls in Best Friends found that one percent said they had been pregnant before high school graduation, compared to 26 percent of their classmates. More recently, among more than 1,600 Best Friend girls nationally only 3% reported having had sexual intercourse, 3% reported having used illegal drugs sometime during their lives; and 76% said that they wanted to wait until marriage to have sex.

Meg Meeker eloquently makes the case that adults must roll up their sleeves and get involved with their teens. She reminds us that while teens may want adult privileges, their reasoning ability and emotional stability are often still those of a child. In spite of their protests to the contrary, they need an abundance of parental involvement in their lives.

That is why I recommend *Restoring the Teenage Soul* for all parents. Reading Meg's book will help you gain a better understanding of your teens and the world in which they live. Arming yourself with this knowledge will certainly help you in guiding and protecting the children you love so much.

ACKNOWLEDGMENTS

THANKS TO WALT, MARY, CHARLOTTE, LAURA, AND WALTER FOR their encouragement and patience during the long hours of writing. Thanks to Mike Yorkey for his wonderful job in editing the manuscript, to Jeff Stoddard for designing the book cover, and to Melissa Cox at the Medical Institute in Austin, Texas, for her input.

Special thanks to my readers: Vickie, Judy, Bob, Lane, and Carol.

And for Margie, Marcus, Darcy, and Freddy, thanks for your beautiful faces.

RESTORING THE TEENAGE SOUL

Chapter One

JESSICA'S STORY

Are those *her* ribs through which the Sun
Did peer, as through a grate?
Is that a DEATH? And are there two?
Is DEATH that woman's mate?

SAMUEL TAYLOR COLERIDGE

THE NURSE HELD JESSICA'S HAND AS SHE SHUFFLED TO THE scale outside the exam room door. My heart went out to the sixteen-year-old girl, whose slight frame was emaciated from months of self-starvation.

I made certain my eyes met the nurse. My nod of the head was understood: I wanted the nurse to ask Jessica to remove her shoes and sweatshirt and take out whatever was in her pockets. Girls with *anorexia nervosa* were known to stuff rocks into their pockets prior to weigh-in. As Jessica stepped up to the scale, I prayed, *Oh, please, Lord, let her have gained just one pound.*

I glanced at the skeleton perched like a lovely bird alighting on a branch in December. She was stiff, frozen. Somehow she looked thinner from fifteen feet than she did up close. I wondered why.

Jessica stepped off the scale and, still coaxed by our nurse, slipped her ninety-eight pounds into the exam room. As I strode down the hall, I wondered if Jessica would be more responsive to the same questions I asked week after week.

"Hi!" I chirped as I entered the brightly lit room. Sitting on the edge of the examination table, her head sagged between her shoulders.

"Hi," she complied.

"How was your weekend?" It was like I was talking to the top of her head.

"Uh, it was okay." The next twenty minutes were long and strenuous, as they always were. As we conversed, I glanced through her chart, excited that her weight was up one pound from her last visit. While I performed the physical exam, I used humorous, compassionate questioning to elicit responses—however muted—from Jessica. I did nothing to confront her, but her body language spoke volumes.

Jessica fixed her eyes upon spots on the carpet. Her frail legs stuck together as though glued, and her baggy shirt-sleeves covered her hands. Presumably she thought her legs were too fat to expose to the world. As our conversation deepened, she drew her knees to her chest, encircling them with her arms. Her speech downshifted to mumbling, and her pitch became almost inaudible. When I questioned her regarding her feelings toward her father or herself, almost on cue she dropped her head even lower.

The posture of *anorexia nervosa* is shame, pain, and self-contempt. Jessica had all three and much more. I felt the examination room fill with sadness—a presence that seemed to penetrate the walls and dominate this frail little teenager.

Jessica was the youngest of two children in a small town. Known as a good kid, she couldn't remember acting out or giving her parents trouble—unlike her older brother. Dad, in the sales business, worked long hours and traveled frequently. He loved her, Jessica remembered —until he divorced Mom, moved to another town, and remarried when she was eleven. She said the divorce never bothered her ("he was gone so much anyway"), but maybe it did—she wasn't quite sure. She, her mother and her brother moved out of their family home and into an apartment. She disliked her new school and wasn't interested in sports. Mom went back to work, relegating Jessica to a latch-key existence, where most afternoons were spent by herself at home with homework, the cat, or TV to entertain her. Day after day she remembers being alone.

Calls from Dad came weekly. He wanted to see her, he said, but his new wife refused to let him visit without her coming along as well. After all, his new wife insisted that she and her husband were "one" now, and that "oneness" included visits with Jessica.

Months passed by. Jessica finally saw her dad with his new wife, but the stepmother was a pain, so Jessica started making up excuses not to visit. When Jessica told me she liked to go shopping with Mom on weekends, I asked if she ever talked with her mother regarding her feelings about her dad. "Not much," she replied. "Mom and Dad never talked much to each other and won't talk to me about how I feel. It's no use."

I tried to probe her about any outside interests that might show some spark—aerobics, jogging, walking, or skiing. She said she never liked sports. And now she had no energy.

Somewhere between four to five months prior to seeing me, Jessica began to diet. She doesn't know why she started, but she said it just felt good. She lost a couple of pounds, liked the results, so she kept going—and going. Her hair began to fall out, her menstruation stopped, and what little interaction she had with school friends became too strained. That's when Mom sought help.

After those first few painful visits, punctuated by stonewall silence, her mother and I watched her weight continue to plummet. Following the incident in which I asked the nurse to check for rocks in her pockets, we decided that Jessica should enter an excellent in-patient hospital program, where she received intensive counseling and interaction with peers who were also suffering from *anorexia nervosa*. At first she refused to eat, but she conceded under threat of liquid feedings via a nasal gastric tube inserted into her nose and down her throat.

"No, I don't want that," she said. "Much too much of an invasion," so she slowly began to eat. She hated food. She felt so desperate to be thin, to not eat, to hold onto that internal terror that repelled food. Jessica even believed she wouldn't mind if starvation killed her. At least she would be in control.

She hated the counselors, the doctors, and the nurses who made her eat. But she always had a choice—the tube or an orange. She hated having that choice.

During her hospital stay, Mom visited for family counseling, and Dad came too. Much to his new wife's distress, he came alone. Even without the dreaded stepmother, Jessica said seeing him made her angry. The anger in her voice was sprinkled with sadness, but I felt she wasn't ready for all her sadness to surface just yet. Part of Jessica's hospitalization included journal writing, an assignment made more difficult, Jessica said, because she didn't like her handwriting. "It's just too ugly," she told me. "Too messy. I'm not a writer, and besides I think it's stupid."

Jessica remained hospitalized almost five weeks. She gained weight well, her heart rate improved, and her hair regained its former luster.

As soon as she returned home from the hospital, Jessica came in for a visit with me. I was excited to see her and her strengthened little body. At first glance, I thought that I detected a hint of a smile on her face, but I was wrong. Jessica was mad. Her face was framed by darting brows and tight lips. Five weeks of hospitalization, and now I had an angry kid on my hands.

Which was not a bad development, I judged. Anger is better than a frozen body filled with frozen emotions. I looked forward to hearing her dissection of that anger.

With the help of excellent counselors, recruitment of her mother's involvement, and frequent visits to our office, Jessica blossomed over the ensuing two years. She grew to become a young woman capable of strong feelings, thinking clearly, a young woman unafraid of her emotions. She had a keener sense of her limitations and the limitations of those she loved. She realized that those limitations didn't need to kill her.

From that first strained visit two years earlier, Jessica had been transformed. Her growth was slow, tedious, and at many times disappointing. But Jessica thrived because one brave adult—her mother—rolled up her sleeves and fought for Jessica. Will she continue to struggle with thoughts of starvation in the future? Probably. But the powerful grip that depression and starvation had over her in those early years has been broken.

ORIGINS OF A DISEASE

Anorexia nervosa—the act of starving oneself to the point of neurosis—has increasingly hit families of every socioeconomic stripe. Originally presenting itself among predominantly upper-middle-class teen girls, *anorexia nervosa* has evolved with the characteristics of a viral infection. *Anorexia* has mutated and masked itself, gripping the psyche of pre-adolescent, teen, and adult women, penetrating some superficially, others to the point of death.

Its roots are often complicated and convoluted, difficult even for the best of psychiatrists, psychologists, and specialized counselors to dissect and heal. Jessica's roots were deep but healable. Now in her twenties, she continues to struggle with food phobia and bouts of self-contempt. But because she trusts the skills of loving adults to enter the depths of her feelings and walk her through them, she is able to redirect her thinking, change her behavior, and hence her feelings. When old feelings of anger and self-hatred surface, she reminds herself that she can choose whether to allow *anorexia* to keep a stronghold on her life. The intervention of a few adults and some peers has helped Jessica see that her hurt, anger, depression, and distorted thinking threatened her body and her well-being.

While Jessica remains a work in progress, I wonder how many other Jessicas are out there struggling, stuck in loneliness, their thoughts deeply contorted by their feelings and the adolescent culture in which they live. These youngsters need adult intervention. *Anorexia nervosa* and *bulimia nervosa* are the outward cries of self-hatred, but in my years of medical practice, I know there are many more subtle symptoms of hurt, anger, and confusion that go unnoticed and unattended. Without adults to stand in the gaps, to help peel back layers of anger, teens may become imbedded in a web of confusion, fear, and even depression. We'll meet one such teen in the next chapter.

Chapter Two

ALLISON'S STORY

But what am I?
An infant crying in the night:
An infant crying for the light:
And with no language but a cry.

ALFRED, LORD TENNYSON

"ALLISON, I KNOW THIS IS TOUGH, BUT I WANT YOU TO TRY. You were in your room, sitting on your bed. Can you tell me what you were thinking, what you were feeling right before you swallowed the pills?"

"Nothing, just nothing, I just wanted to die. What a pain. I wish I had."

The next minutes were long and thick with silence. My helplessness was palpable. Exhuming feelings buried beneath numbness takes time, patience, and delicate skills. Unfortunately, kids like Allison come into my office with increasing frequency; not because of who I am or my expertise, but because the number of broken teens has become more numerous than ever in the past decade.

For the most part, they are teens with nowhere to go. Their parents don't know what to do with their problems: the most fundamental of "right behaviors," having fused with "wrong behaviors," are reshaping ethical behavior into nonexistence. Teachers, particularly those working in special education, spend less time teaching and more time troubleshooting aberrant teen behaviors to maintain classroom order. Psychologists' and counselors' offices are often overburdened with long waiting lists.

Allison has a family: until a couple of years ago, she lived at home with her siblings and her mother and attended our local public high school. She says her biggest problem is depression, but adds that she just doesn't know what to do about it. In fact, she says, since coming to the halfway home for girls in which she presently resides, she feels her depression has improved.

I return to my original question regarding her feelings surrounding her suicide attempt six weeks earlier, sensing an eagerness as she tries to review the incident. But after several attempts to recount the event—attempts with certain levels of comfort and safety—she sincerely can't unlock any feelings.

Allison is numb, and she is only sixteen. "Are you still smoking?" I tried.

"Oh, I quit because it was making me feel so sick. I'm gay you know."

"Oh," I responded. "What makes you say that?"

"I dunno—I just hate men and I like being with women better."

"Allison, are you sexually active with girls your age or other women?" I probed.

"Oh no, I don't want to do that. I just hate men."

"What makes you hate men so?" I asked, realizing that I had hit a nerve.

Her eyes hit the floor, and I received no response. Silence cloaked her, and if shame had a facial expression, she would have worn it. She didn't have to tell me why she hated men. I knew, but I wanted her to tell me. It wasn't her dad or her brother but a stepdad who, three years earlier, entered the privacy of her room and the holiness of her body and shredded her heart with the claws of his distorted sexual and hostile drives.

At that moment (and each ensuing episode), the sexuality of a little girl was maimed and hopelessly knotted. The problem was that Allison didn't know this. All she knew was that she felt numb—and hated men.

"You have reason to hate men," I empathized. "Can you tell me what happened?" Silence. I knew the story because her mother had revealed the truth to me earlier. But Allison could not allow to have the truth forced on her like her stepfather's sexual urges; she needed to come out with it on her timetable.

Realizing that she trusted neither herself nor me yet with disclosure of any deep feelings, I journeyed toward a mechanical discussion on the psychology of depression with Allison. She understood, as best she could, but understanding didn't make her feel any better. With little interactive conversation ensuing, I continued discoursing about the perceptions of pain through sexual abuse and the resulting confusion about her sexuality, her needs, and her self-esteem.

Allison remained confused, and the truth is, she should have been confused. As much as Allison tries on her own, her confusion will remain and deepen if she doesn't receive diligent and supportive guidance by significant adults in her life. I didn't tell her that she stood a very high statistical probability of remaining confused and broken if she was not willing to risk her heart with an adult in her life who could help guide her toward healing.

Allison won't be quite sure what she wants to do about her sexual relationships. As a matter of fact, she said she finds lesbianism quite distasteful and confusing. Since she hates men, ergo, she had just decided to be gay. This was good, she said, because then she wouldn't have to worry about becoming pregnant, about dealing with men, about all those feelings that get stirred up.

I asked Allison to describe a typical day at the girls' home, where she now lives.

"Oh, I study a little, talk with the girls. We sometimes get into arguments. Best of all, I like to watch TV," she allowed.

"What do you like to watch?"

"Oh, it doesn't matter: MTV, 'Matlock,' 'Fresh Prince,' whatever's on."

From a short recitation of her favorite television shows and stars, I diligently but gently tried to circle back to her depression.

"Did you watch much television when you lived at home?" I started.

"Of course I did. Mom and I used to watch TV a lot together. That is—when she was around. The first time she left I watched a whole lot of TV; I just didn't know what else to do," Allison responded, warming up somewhat.

"Can you tell me about that first time—when she left?" I tried.

"I've already told you." Her eyes refused to focus on any part of my body, hoping that I—and my questions—would disappear from the room. Then, perhaps, the reality of her past would be simply a bad dream.

"I know, Allie, I just want you to tell me again." This was the last question I needed to ask during the next minutes. She was ready, and she began outlining the events that so wounded her.

She was only nine at the time, living at home with her mother and her nine-month-old baby brother. Her mother drank herself to drunkenness one evening, then decided she could no longer "cope," so she took off into the darkness. Allison was left home alone for two days and nights with her baby brother, too afraid to leave the house or call for help. She had no older siblings, and her stepdad had long since gone. Besides, she would never call him anyway.

Allison survived those days as best she could, her feelings dulled. Even after her mother came to her senses and returned home, Allison continued to be afraid. *When would she leave again?* Since she didn't know, Allison did not sleep well or perform well in school. The second time her mom disappeared, Allison said, she did something that she says she'll never forgive herself for.

"What was that?" I asked.

Silence stayed with us for several moments, but she was ready to reveal the action that happened seven years earlier.

"I really didn't mean to—I didn't really want to, but maybe I did." She broke down sobbing. I was grateful for her tears. Finally, healing was meandering its way into her life.

"That's okay," I soothed. "You're all right now."

"I was so scared, and I hated my baby brother. I didn't want him to be there so I put a pillow over his head for a long time. I hated him, but I didn't kill him. I stopped. But I hated myself for trying to kill him. Mom doesn't know—you won't tell her, will you?"

"No, Allison, I won't tell your mother." Allison cried many minutes, and I sat and waited for her to get it all out, glad for a heart that felt again, wishing at times that mine weren't so sensitive.

I ran through her chart: by age sixteen, Allison had been abandoned and reunited repeatedly with her broken mother, attempted murder, been sexually assaulted by her stepfather, been absconded by police for delinquent behavior, and most recently had attempted suicide.

Was there hope for Allison?

Yes, I believed so, otherwise I would have to retire from practice. I am not a psychiatrist, but a pediatrician—seeing many of the kids who never make it for a variety of reasons to the psychiatrists' offices.

Allison can heal, if she has adults who will intercede for her, persevere with her, help her progress, and stay with her. Adults who will reach down with her into the recesses of her heart and mind to begin restoring her. Her peers can't do it because this is best left to those with experience, as you'll soon see in the next chapter.

Chapter Three

MICHAEL'S STORY

~

"**H**OW'S SENIOR YEAR GOING?" I QUERIED AS I BEGAN MY physical exam on Michael.

"Oh, pretty well—but you know, I feel tired a lot. My mom wanted me to ask you about that. I'm just tired all the time. I don't know what's wrong with me."

Michael proceeded to outline his days in response to my request. He awoke at 6 a.m. and was at school by 7:30 a.m., taking five classes each day. After school he met up with his track team and practiced for two hours. Then he went home, ate, studied, or worked two nights at a fast-food restaurant. On weekends he either attended track meets or worked behind the counter taking orders, sometimes both.

"It sounds to me like something has to give, Mike. You have no down time scheduled. No wonder you're tired," I suggested.

As I went through his list of daily activities, I questioned which ones could be curbed. His job, no—that money was earmarked for college. Take easier classes? No, that wouldn't work—those were college prep classes. Track? "No way," he exhorted. "I run all year 'round. My parents come to every meet—they've never missed one."

Since I knew his parents, I knew Michael was telling the truth. Before track, he was going to be the next Larry Bird on the basketball court until he stopped growing. Now in his senior year, he no longer felt so excited about track because he was just tired—too tired for an eighteen-year-old, I believed.

I continued to probe about his track commitment and realized that he felt guilty about wanting to scale back on his training. His parents loved watching him run, only natural since he was their only son. In fact, Mom and Dad loved watching him run too much, cheerfully waiting long hours between his events. Their enthusiasm reflected their desire for him to succeed, and running made him feel more important to them.

Our conversation took a left turn when I asked Michael about his girlfriend of two years.

"Are you still seeing Adrianna?" I began.

"Oh, yeah. We've been seeing each other a lot lately," he answered.

"What kinds of things do you do together?" I probed.

"Oh, just about anything. We talk a lot. She's great to talk to. When I'm not getting along with my folks or school's driving me crazy, I talk to Adrianna. She's just so understanding. I can talk to her about anything."

"Does she come to your track meets?" I asked.

"Well, whenever she can. Problem is she works after school, too. Sometimes she's there, sometimes she's not. It's okay," Michael continued, obviously enjoying talking about Adrianna.

"I'm really going to miss her when I leave for college this fall," he continued without prompting. "I wish she weren't a year behind me: then we could go to the same school." As he spoke these words, the tension between his affection for Adrianna and the guilt over his desires for her became evident in his tone and facial expression.

"Have you talked about sex with her?" I asked.

"Oh, yeah. And we've decided it's wrong before marriage so we're going to wait." His voice was firm but I detected uncertainty and struggle. Not in his belief system, since I knew him and his family well, but in his ability to resist the temptation that his desires presented.

"Is sexual restraint hard for the two of you?" I felt comfortable asking this deeper question.

"You know, Dr. Meeker, it really is. I didn't know it was going to be so hard. I know we shouldn't have sex, but I guess I really want to, although I shouldn't want to."

His surprise for talking so openly took over, and I could tell that he wanted to end the conversation.

"So who do you talk to about this?" I asked, not wanting the subject to die.

"No one," he replied.

"Not even your father or close friends?" I asked.

"Nope."

"Do you want to or would you consider talking to your dad about it?" I suggested.

"No way, I just couldn't, and I know he wouldn't want to either."

I came to the sad realization that his father really wouldn't want to, and even if he did, embarrassment might prevent him from addressing the subject head-on. But unless one significant adult was courageous enough to embrace and guide Michael's sexuality, untangle his frustrated feelings and desires, he would continue to teeter between "should I or shouldn't I?", falling prey to a culture screaming: "Yes, you should."

Eighteen-year-old Michael was confused, lonely, and feeling guilty. He was confused about the choices facing him regarding his relationship with Adrianna. Unfortunately, these choices carried tough consequences, and he needed help figuring out what was best for him. Teens like Michael have always struggled with these issues, but there are consequences to premarital sexual behavior, which are more serious than ever.

Michael—track star, excellent student and soon-to-be-college student—needed help. While his immediate social concerns and emotional issues are different from Allison's and Jessica's, he yearned for guidance and teaching as much as they did.

But what exactly do these three need? They need clear direction in a confusing world that has discouraged many young adults to the point of submissive paralysis. These young people need help from those of us who can come alongside and help them progress toward emotional, physical, and spiritual health. The adults in their lives—parents, teachers and health professionals such as me—have failed them because we are confused and frightened. We have transferred our fears of the emotional and physical health issues facing them (drug and alcohol use, teen pregnancy, depression) into fear of teens themselves. Many of us are parenting on the heels of the sexual revolution of the sixties and seventies, which has our moral compasses all aflutter.

Many of us like Allison's mother have failed our teens and believe (erroneously) that we cannot restore our kids. This is a lie. As far as our kids are concerned, the time for restoration is never too late.

I have alluded to groups of adults—perhaps two or three—needed in this process. This may include a mom or dad, an aunt or an uncle, a teacher, a family friend, or some other significant adult. We need adults strong enough to come "under" teens, willing to understand their needs and help direct the choices that they will make. We need adults to help them grow into emotionally, physically, and spiritually sound young adults. We must be willing to look into their minds and their hearts clearly to understand their fundamental needs. Then we must see how teens attempt to have these needs met.

Finally, we must have the strength to examine ourselves by asking some hard questions: Can we meet those needs? Do we want to? Are we willing to sacrifice to do so? If we feel that we are not meeting these needs, why aren't we?

This process is not for the feeble-hearted, but it is one that can literally give life to teens, and amazingly enough, life to parents as well. Let's take a look into the hearts of teens.

Chapter Four

WHAT DO TEENS NEED?

THREE TEENS FROM THE SAME TOWN LIVING IN DIFFERENT
worlds:

- ❖ Jessica, compliant and quiet, comfortable with aloneness, uncomfortable with feeling, so disturbed by life that she decided to change things even if it cost her her life.
- ❖ Allison, five miles away in a bedroom at a halfway home, raging at the wallpaper because "it was there."
- ❖ Michael, struggling with an adolescent culture assaulting him with images of manhood, sexuality, and expectations.

It is my conviction that these three teens with markedly different backgrounds and problems have common needs. While it would not serve the sophistication of psychology fields to state that the meeting of these common needs would blunt the trauma and pain that each experienced, I submit that we as a culture of caring adults must begin somewhere to restore integrity and emotional health to our teens.

Certainly, healing for Allison takes more intricate psychological discernment than for Michael, but we must look back into their lives, peer through the web of pain heaped onto their fragile souls, and strengthen them. Otherwise, I fear, there will be no hope.

My purpose in the ensuing discussions is not to undermine necessary applications of sophisticated psychological technique. My purpose is to simplify teen needs into a workable, understandable fashion for adults who are intent on helping teens. We will peek into their minds and their hearts in order that we may intercede for them. Teens, because of limitations of intellectual development, are unable to intercede for themselves and for one another. We adults must know what we're doing before we can come under them.

Jessica suffered from *anorexia nervosa,* a broken family, depression, and a poor sense of her value as a person. The expression of starvation pointed toward a need to control—or change—something in her life in hopes of feeling better about who she was. Her severe starvation, however, arrested a part of herself that was beginning to mature. While her body blossomed into puberty, a deeper emotional part of her was terrified about growing up. I could tell just by her posture in those early visits: curled into a fetal position, back facing front. A little girl within a little girl, afraid of life, afraid of feeling, afraid of being. There existed a part of her that felt unsafe for a variety of reasons.

Careful speculation of her prior years revealed a profound lack of intimacy in Jessica's life. There was no physical or emotional intimacy modeled between Mom and Dad before the marriage dissolved, and certainly there was no sense of intimacy between Jessica and Dad or Jessica and Mom.

Now let's look at Allison. Her life was a bona fide mess, and at casual glance, one might become too overwhelmed to simplify her unmet needs. First, she had no sense of family that gifted her with any type of love. Many kids in this situation, reared by parents too sick to actually love them (and I have experienced parents who really say they just don't love their kids), can survive if they fabricate love. They imagine their parents to be someone they are not in order that they will perceive love. For certain, if children cannot even perceive being loved—the most fundamental of human needs—they might as well not live.

Allison "idealized" her mother to be one who loved her, but there was no safety for her in seeing this love because Allison never knew when her mom would be there or when she would take off. Certainly, her own sense of value was skewed when her mom left her all alone for two days. This event caused the nine-year-old to wonder why she was not worthy of her mother's care. Her identity quickly changed from child to caretaker, as she was forced to feed, clothe, and care for a nine-month baby unable to do anything for himself. Finally, her sense of intimacy—of being touched and loved—was perverted by her stepfather's sexual assaults.

Michael, we might conclude, has nothing in common with either of these two. He wasn't depressed, wasn't starving, and hadn't been sexually assaulted. He seemed to have been functioning quite well. But attention to Michael's needs are as necessary—if not more so—since his needs are more subtle than the other two. For a "normal teen" immersed in a culture that assaults him with the disguised notion that quick, cheap substitutes exist for meeting his needs, this development can literally kill him with one wrong move. Never has a culture been so anti-teen, so willing to strangle the life and soul out of healthy kids.

Michael appeared to be one of the "normal" kids. He ran track, thrived in a family of relatively normal parents, enjoyed a sense of who he was and how he "fit" into his family structure. He said he knew his parents loved him, but more importantly he drew from their love to perform volunteer work with his church in underprivileged areas. Charitable work enhanced his sense of self and bolstered his identity as a compassionate young man capable of working and serving the less fortunate.

While Michael understood a sense of his own worth, emotionally there was little room in his home to feel his feelings. In short, Michael's home lacked "emotional safety." Michael felt intimidated to be angry, frustrated, or sad at times. Whenever he expressed any feelings of anger, he described to me that his father would become angrier. Michael's response to his domineering manner was to close up and to allow his own feelings to dive beneath the surface.

This news did not surprise me; I have experienced this child-parent emotional dynamic quite frequently. Michael's father would become frustrated with his anger and react in the only fashion he knew.

When it came to expressing sadness and hurt, Michael fared better with his mother. He still felt less than comfortable divulging his deep feelings, pulling back if Mom attempted to probe. Between Michael, Mom, and Dad, an emptiness hung: no one was quite sure how the other really felt. For Michael, experiencing the excitement of a girlfriend and the temptations to engage in sexual activity, his options were limited to recruit parental involvement in his decision-making. His parents would have liked to help him work through his decisions with his girlfriend, but they were uncomfortable discussing their feelings. It was precisely this discomfort that disallowed emotional safety in Michael's home.

Intimacy, love, a sense of value, and safety are the four fundamental needs evidenced in the lives of these three teens. The meeting of these four needs is, I believe, the foundation of complete health for all teens—both female and male.

A LOOK AT INTIMACY

Those who have parented children through all developmental stages into adulthood might balk at the notion that teens require intimacy. For rebellious, independent teens refusing to want any involvement in family activities, intimacy may seem to be the last thing they need.

Don't lose sight, however, that teens are akin to toddlers in adult clothes. While their needs evolve and mature, their outward expressions may fool us. What is intimacy, and how does it affect teens?

Intimacy is the need for connectedness between two people. During this connectedness, three very important events occur. First, a part of the self (the teen self in this case) is opened and revealed. Second, the receiver sees what is opened and makes a decision about what he sees, albeit a subconscious one. Finally, that part of the self that has been revealed and offered is either embraced or rejected.

Intimacy for younger children is much easier since they are less inhibited to reveal themselves. For example, toddlers cry easily ("I am afraid") and readily hug ("I need affection"). Parents see the emotion (fear, for example) revealed, determine that the child's need to have his fears calmed is real, and thus embrace him by giving him a hug.

By the time adolescence creeps in, however, enough rejection has occurred over the years that teens raise their defenses and forbid certain parts of their selves to be revealed again, lest they feel painful rejection once more. Intimacy requires vulnerability. One cannot be received if one is not first opened and revealed.

Thus, the first part of intimacy requires a sense of willingness on the teen's part to avail herself to being seen, to being opened for scrutiny. When the opening takes place ("I will allow you to see this part of who I am") and she has a pleasant experience ("You like what I have shown you"), intimacy has occurred.

When children have pleasant experiences of connectedness and intimacy with parents and significant older adults, an increased sense of security and identity begins to emerge and flourish. But when they experience disconnection on the receiving end ("You don't approve of who I am and fail to embrace me") they are emotionally thrown off balance.

Teens need connectedness as much as toddlers and young children. They need intimacy, particularly during the teen years when they are testing who they are and where they fit in. They stray, pull back from the initial point of reference of intimacy (the family) to figure out how intimacy inside the family unit feels compared to intimacy outside the family unit. If intimacy within the family structure (Mom,

Dad, and siblings) has been a positive and strengthening experience, a teen feels less needy to experience intimacy on a deeper level outside the family unit.

This does not mean that healthy teens won't desire to spend more time with peers than with the family. Wanting more time with peers is part of healthy teen separation and development. The difference between healthy teen interaction with peers and unhealthy interaction stems from the neediness a teen may feel within that peer group. A teen who experiences genuine connectedness at home will be less needy for intimacy from the group than the teen who craves intimacy. Healthy intimacy occurs for teens when all three stages of intimacy—opening the self, scrutiny of the self by observer, and acceptance of the self—have been successfully completed.

Essentially, intimacy can be experienced on three different levels: emotional intimacy, physical intimacy, and spiritual intimacy.

EMOTIONAL INTIMACY

Emotional intimacy is the connectedness of feelings. In the early years, revealing of emotions within the home comes naturally for children. They scream, laugh, and cry quite easily. Parents see the emotions and respond appropriately for the most part. If a child cries, we comfort him; if he screams, we calm him down and ask what's wrong. The child-parent connection and intimacy are more naturally completed with sharing and acceptance of those feelings.

As the teen years approach, the child senses an appropriate deepening and broadening of emotions. He has feelings for a girlfriend, a deeper hurt because Dad criticizes his athletic ability, and furor that Mom won't allow him to roam until 1 a.m. His emotions feel deeper and more complex, and intimacy seems more frightening. Depending upon his previous experience with exposing his emotions, he will either continue to reveal what he feels or he won't.

Parenting teens and meeting intimacy needs can be quite tricky.

Teens may be confused about the number and depth of their emotions (which is why they are not sure how to express them), and parents simply may fail to accept these feelings. Let's face it: it's hard to see teenagers frustrated, angry, or in pain, which is why we may feel uncomfortable with the emotions erupting from teens. Thus parents, as well as teens, block the exchange of intimacy.

On the other hand, teens are often hesitant to be vulnerable in opening their hearts with parents for a variety of reasons. First of all, they may feel that since they are maturing, they should be able to handle their own feelings. To them, "handling their feelings" means keeping them locked inside. This is difficult and can sometimes prove "crazy making" for teens because they experience such new and conflicting feelings.

Second, they may fear rejection if they share their feelings. They are terrified of looking "stupid" and are familiar enough with rejection to want to avoid it in areas that feel significant to them.

Teens developmentally have a need to stay rooted in their connectedness with their mothers and fathers. Therefore, they fear disrupting this security by being vulnerable to share their emotions if there is any doubt that those emotions will be accepted. This statement might sound crazy, particularly to parents who have boisterous and outspoken teenagers and are struggling to restrain their teens' tongues.

Remember, we are discussing genuine emotional intimacy—the availing of a teen's heart, wherein he allows himself to be vulnerable with regard to his deep feelings, followed by an acceptance of those feelings by a parent or other significant adult. What about teens who mouth off at parents? Are they attempting intimacy? No, they are displaying frustration and fear.

Teens who lack intimacy with an adult search anywhere for a substitute. Unsatiated intimacy, particularly emotional intimacy, drives teens to connect somewhere. When they "find" intimacy outside of the home, they actually feel even more frustrated because their need for deeper intimacy with a parent wasn't completely filled. They press forward in a craving fashion, trying again and again to find it.

The cycle of seeking, not being satisfied, and seeking again persists. Freud dubbed this "repetition-compulsion" in its most severe form. Teens search over and over for emotional intimacy when it is not found at home.

PHYSICAL INTIMACY

Physical intimacy is the need that teens have for healthy touch. When teens are not hugged, stroked on the head, or held in their parents' arms, they search for a substitute—usually the arms of someone from the opposite sex.

Can there be any doubt? Look at the teen pregnancy rates. We adults persist in discussing the high teen pregnancy and sexual activity rates, but as someone who speaks with teens on a regular basis, conversing openly and honestly with them in my office, there can be no doubt in my mind that deeper emotional and physical needs drive their sexual activity as much as, and probably more so, than hormones.

All human beings need touch because it reminds us that we are desirable, lovable, and worthy. The opposite of intimacy is aloneness, an experience that prompts a barrage of feelings, some of which are among the most profound and painful in the human experience. Abandonment, for instance, is excruciating for teens. A teen caught in an abandonment situation asks herself: *Am I alone because I am not worthy of Mom or Dad's love?*

Typically teens who experience loneliness blame themselves since they are developmentally egocentric. *If I am alone*, she presumes, *I must deserve it because of something I said or did.* Physical intimacy on the most fundamental level reassures her that she is worthy of love and connectedness. *If you touch me, I exist and I am worthy of being touched, worthy of not being alone,* is what she is feeling.

Anyone who has parented teens recognizes quickly that many resist being touched. One commentator likened hugging his reluctant teen to hugging a telephone pole! Most teens are painfully uncomfortable with their bodies. Teen girls and boys alike either feel too fat, too thin, or too weak. Spend fifteen minutes talking with a teen, and you will learn which part of his body he dislikes. If a teen dislikes part of his physique, he is certain that you, the adult, will dislike it as well. When he feels unsure, he recoils from touch altogether.

It's easy, then, to conclude that touching and hugging is for youngsters, but this is far from the truth. Teens have a need for physical connectedness that is real and deep, despite their outward behavior. As a matter of fact, touch is necessary now more than ever as their sexuality emerges and flourishes.

SPIRITUAL INTIMACY

Why do we talk about restoring the soul of teens? Historically, the soul has had two connotations. The soul can either be the "seat of the emotions," or it can be that part of the human that is imperishable, invisible—connected to a world that we cannot see.

As a physician who has had thousands of conversations with emotionally and physically sick teens, I cannot easily carve the physical and emotional parts from the spiritual dimensions of illnesses. Sometimes these ailments can be isolated from one another, but sometimes they cannot. While I would not venture to neatly compartmentalize the "spiritual" dimension of any physical or emotional illness, I simply report the element of intimacy that teens have expressed to me.

What is spiritual intimacy? I define spiritual intimacy as an exchange of feelings and experiences with God. It includes the giving of feelings and thoughts to an invisible deity, believing that God receives them and responds back.

The existence of children's spirituality is supported in Robert Coles' book *The Spiritual Life of Children*. Woven throughout his work are children's perceptions of God—His face, His voice, His character. Clearly, at a very early age, children are open to seeing and experiencing the unseen. My personal work with teens has led me to conclude that teens are perhaps more open to their spirituality because it is exciting and recruits intellectual energy. Spirituality is part of the lives of many of my teen patients, and as such must be acknowledged and attended to.

Thus, spiritual intimacy is the availing of oneself to the deeper, to the unseen. Is there an appropriate response as this part of self is unveiled? Can spiritual intimacy exist?

Michael explained his own experience of spiritual intimacy. His parents raised him in a Christian church, teaching him the fundamentals regarding the existence of God and the Trinity. Sunday school brought him knowledge and facts. Sermons bored him, however, and his Wednesday night youth group often required his parent's insistence regarding attendance.

Michael loved his parents and enjoyed their company. While they took him to church and church meetings regularly, they allowed him freedom as he grew through adolescence to review his own relationship with God and separate it from their relationship with God. This was critical in his experience of intimacy with God because intimacy can never be obtained secondhand. It must be real and personal, and to Michael, God was.

The reason I believe that Michael experienced intimacy on a spiritual level was because it was genuine and true to him. That truth and intimacy provided an emotional and spiritual platform from which he could act and compare other life experiences. Spiritual intimacy gave life to Michael.

Henri Nouwen, a recently deceased Catholic priest and master with the pen, described similar experiences regarding intimacy with God. In the pages of his book, *The Genessee Diary*, he recorded descriptions of his feelings and conversations with God. Through recruitment of his intellectual brilliance and his belief in an invisible God, he availed part of himself—his feelings and his body—to engage in a relationship with God.

Father Nouwen's writings revealed his trust in an invisible God to accept and receive a deep part of him. "Indeed prayer is the only real way to clean my heart and to create new space," he wrote. "I am discovering how important that inner space is. When I sense that inner quiet peace, I can pray for many others and feel a very intimate relationship with them. Now I know that it is not I who prays but the spirit of God who prays in me. Indeed, when God's glory dwells in me, there is nothing too far away, nothing too painful, nothing too strange or too familiar that it cannot contain and renew by its touch. Every time I recognize the glory of God in me and give it space to manifest itself to me, all that is human can be brought there and nothing will be the same again."[1]

The priest has no doubt that God hears his prayers. "All questions about 'the social relevance of prayer' seem dull and very unintelligent to me. I've found that the silent prayer of the monks is one of the few things that keeps some sanity in this world."[2]

Father Nouwen's writings reveal his trust in an invisible God to accept and receive a deep part of himself. Interestingly, the priest described receiving back something from God—experiences that substantiate the existence of spiritual intimacy in his life. This is the same intimacy that Michael and other teens have described to me.

Dr. David Allen, a Harvard-educated psychiatrist, comments on spirituality in *Shattering the Gods Within*. Dr. Allen writes, "Human beings are religious persons, and frequently the search for the transcendence leads to a more purposeful life. Paul Tillich claimed that the search for ultimate meaning is the central theme of human existence."[3]

I submit that a sense of spirituality—a curiosity regarding the unseen—exists in many teens. During one of Allison's appointments, she lifted her baseball cap to reveal a series of silver shapes marching up her earlobe. One was a cross, and I remarked on it to probe her spirituality. "So tell me about your earrings—the cross in particular. Does it mean anything, or is it just a decoration?"

"Oh, I don't know—just a decoration," she replied.

"What about God or a life beyond what we see? What do you think?" I posed.

"No, I believe when you die, you die. Besides, if there is a God, He can't be very nice. He's sure never been around for me." Her tone became icier. I paused and examined her joints before she started again.

"Well, I've tried praying," she offered. "I don't get it when people say God answers your prayers—he never hears me. I would pray and pray, but my mom never stopped drinking. I just gave up on God. He must not think much of me."

Interestingly, Allison had perceived a spiritual dimension to her life. She had prayed. She had reached beyond her self, beyond her mother's drinking, and sought out someone deeper, more loving, more perfect who might help. In spite of her professed lack of belief, she believed in spirituality and had sought spiritual intimacy. Had she been schooled? I don't think so. I believe her reaching out to God came intuitively, as naturally as her longing for connection with her mother.

Spiritual intimacy, connecting with an invisible God, makes sense in the lives of teens. They are vulnerable to explore the deeper and unseen, finding intellectual and emotional excitement. Spirituality, after all, is another new dimension in their growing world, a longing to be accepted and loved when receipt of such is fractured or nonexistent in their visible world.

Younger children write and speak freely to God. Letters that children write to God reveal a willingness to allow examination of their thoughts and feelings. Perhaps they are more open to a Supreme

Being because they have received less rejection in their short lives. I believe that their perceptions of God are also less tarnished. Their limited experience with human adults allows them to see God as He is rather than as an extension of Mom or Dad.

Teens, on the other hand, may be less open to God. If they have experienced rejection and hurt from human adults, they in turn superimpose that image onto God, distorting His character from all-loving to just another mean adult, which Allison had done.

If teens have had negative experiences with adults, they may be less open to spiritual experiences with God. On the other hand, it may be the very turmoil of life that encourages them toward spiritual intimacy. Regardless of the motive, many teens seek intimacy on a spiritual level, as well as love, as we'll explore in the next chapter.

Chapter Five

LOVE:
GIVING AND RECEIVING

NOTHING SHOULD SEEM MORE NATURAL TO THE HUMAN EXIStence than the giving and receiving of love. We are a culture craving love, a culture trying harder and more frantically to experience love with emotional depth and stability. We try so hard that we divorce and remarry, see the right counselors, and become involved in church and self-help groups to find help in receiving and experiencing love.

Our teens' desire to give and receive love is more intuitive, so let's look at it from their perspective.

The experience of love requires two individuals and embodies two components: giving love and receiving love. For teens, giving love is more natural and less risky than receiving love.

Since the experience of love is so integral to all human beings, teens continue to recognize their own need to be in love relationships. But since their world is expanding and new tensions arise between them and their parents, they experiment with giving love to individuals other than their parents.

Giving Love

To most teens giving love feels good: it is exciting and affirming. Giving love to those outside their familiar circle enhances their sense of independence and even their self-worth. Teen girls experiment with love-giving techniques.

Boys experiment and give love differently than girls, who, for instance, are more relationally oriented. They need relationships with girlfriends and boys (as friends), and frequent verbal conversation is their usual medium for love expression. Hence, that's why we see extra phone lines in the homes of teen girls. Talking is an expression of love for them, an arena for the discovery of self-perception. Conversation for teen girls is extremely healthy since it's often a place where love is returned.

Teen boys, on the other hand, may be more pragmatic and service-oriented in their expression of love. Wired with less relational needs, they may extend love to parents, friends, or girlfriends by mowing the lawn, finishing homework on time, hanging out together, or giving gifts. Their discomfort with a physique failing to claim full manhood renders them less likely to touch or hug a parent. As a matter of fact, boys may outwardly disdain physical touch but inwardly crave it.

Parents, please, keep hugging them, even if you feel they lack any interest in being touched. Astute parents can usually discern differences among children regarding their particular style of giving love. This requires objectivity, time, and intuitive observation, but finding your teen's particular manner of love expression pays off.

These expressions are usually cloaked with layers of disguise (lest a teen look like a "wimpy" kid), but it will make you feel a lot better about your child's real need for a love relationship with you. Discovering your teen's particular manner of expressing love is just as important for you as it is for him. Much of a parent's pain and difficulty with the teen years stems from a sudden experience of feeling unloved as well as unneeded. Not feeling needed is hard to cope with, but feeling unloved cuts to a deeper level.

Understand that teens do love parents and need to love parents, but their perception of that love has changed. Their love feels confusing to them because they don't feel it at times and may be convinced they don't love their parents.

What is happening inside the teen's heart is the maturing of love from a feeling to a behavior. The mature adult understands that love is more than a feeling. Love is also an action. A parent's role is to first understand this evolution and then aid the teen by teaching the broader concept of love as a feeling *and* a behavior.

Why is it important for parents to identify particular expressions of their teens' love? Because it reassures parents that indeed their teens still love them, which helps us feel better, more secure, and more equipped to parent effectively.

Perhaps many reading this will struggle with the notion that their teens love them at all. Remember, teens need to love and the young child within them reminds them that they need to give and receive love from you, the parent. This exchange of love drives their behavior. The power of this parent-child interaction may heighten in intensity as they struggle with pulling away.

THE LOVE TUG OF WAR

During the early childhood years, kids naturally give love to their parents, but as children reach the teen years, they become more uncomfortable as their sense of independence emerges. They think, *How can I love someone that I'm trying to pull away from?* This can be frightening for teens and cause them to reject their need to express love to their parents.

In addition, they may experience for the first time the power of two contradicting emotions standing side by side. For instance, a teen may love his dad but hate him at the same time because he won't let him stay out past midnight. A teen girl may recognize her need to love Mom but feel angry at a mother who works long hours and is unavailable to talk to her.

Cognitively, teens develop abstract thinking during the later teen years, which are between fifteen and eighteen years of age. During early adolescence, concrete forms of thinking still operate, and young teens view relationships in a black-and-white manner. They feel as though their parents either love them or hate them. Concrete thought patterns prevent them from understanding parents as friends.

When love exists alongside anger within the teens' heart, the confusion can be overwhelming. They are unable to reconcile this phenomenon, particularly since it is often subconscious. They act out against the parent, testing, searching for a side to take. *Can I love you or should I hate you?* Hence the tug of war begins. *Will you, my dear parent, love me or hate me? Certainly you can't do both.*

When teens are frustrated, they act out in obnoxious and defiant ways. Parents unaware of the internal struggle often take their teens' behavior personally and react out of their own sense of rejection and hurt. Remember, however, that the tug of war may not be the parent's fault because the teen's new awareness of love and anger can result in an overwhelming sense of frustration and confusion.

Parents who can recognize the internal struggle expressed as an outward tug of war and who can resist taking this internal struggle personally will greatly ease the pain of the teen years. Standing back and watching, supporting and consistently giving firm guidelines (which will probably evoke more anger in teens) will enhance a teen's ability to mature through this emotional process.

Restoring the teen soul requires a willingness to help teens struggle with hard emotional and intellectual issues and sort out how one impacts the other. When teens feel love, they perceive the power of the feelings and believe that these feelings are so powerful that they dictate their behavior and their thinking. In fact, many adults feel this way, too.

But healthy parenting and a desire to restore teens to a sense of freedom and dignity necessitates an ability to help teens feel, think, and then separate their feelings from their behavior. This concept, which we will delve into more thoroughly in a later chapter, is vital to establishing healthy maturity and a sense of healthy empowerment in a teen's life.

RECEIVING LOVE

Giving and expressing love can be confusing for teens, but receiving love can be even tougher. Taking love from a parent, close friend, or relative is much riskier than giving love.

Why is this? Because humans can give something away without needing it. But receiving love implies that we need it, even desire it; thus it has an influential power in our lives. Admitting that we need love can be painful, particularly to people (teens) who have experienced recurrent rejection. They say: *If I need love, and I open myself to receive it, what will happen if Mom or Dad doesn't want to give it?*

Receiving love feels very risky for teens, and indeed it is. If she opens herself to take love, then what happens if love isn't given—or not given the way she feels it should be given? The teen's response is to assume responsibility for the lack of love exchange: *If I open myself to take Mom or Dad's love and they reject me, I must be unlovable, or I must have done something wrong.*

Emotionally, their myopic focus upon the self controls the sense of responsibility they feel for all that goes awry in their lives. When it comes to infractions in receiving love, self-contempt can take over, shaking the teen's deepest sense of security. She speculates, *If Mom and Dad don't want to give me love, then I must really be rotten.* This thinking is egocentric, reflecting her inability to meaningfully see that perhaps the problem lies outside of herself—in other words with Mom or Dad. Her thinking goes something like this: *I need love. I recognize that need. That need is not being met. I hate you, Mom, for not meeting it. I hate that I need love. I hate myself.*

KNOWING YOUR CHARACTER

Most parents can remember their toddler unabashedly striking up a conversation with a complete stranger. Young children worry less about what teachers or other adults may think of them, allowing them to be more open to free exchanges.

Teenagers, on the other hand, are much more cautious in their exchanges with significant adults. They hold back with adults, particularly if they recognize they have to get something from the adult. Teens care what adults think, need their approval, and want love from them. But teens have been around long enough to realize that not all adults give them what they want or need, which makes them become selective about their interactions.

When teens' perceptive skills mature, they enjoy a new sense of understanding the characters of adults. They are learning to "read" adults and make decisions about their involvement with adults according to what they perceive. If teens view honesty and consistency in an adult, they will wait to see if these qualities persist.

If they do, then the teen will make a decision about whether the adult is "safe" to open up to. Opening may be talking to the adult more, spending more time together, or helping with chores. As the teen ventures toward any of these overtures, he is testing the adult's character to see if he or she is safe enough to take love from. His testing teaches him more about the adult's character, giving him red lights or green lights regarding his pursuit of interaction with them.

If the teen recognizes the adult's character as honest and safe, he will pursue the possibility of receiving love from him or her. If he senses rejection, he will turn away. Rather than turning quietly, he will vent his rejection with obnoxious behavior. Teens who have experienced rejection from significant adults try to act as unlovable as possible, thus fulfilling the prophesy they espoused.

TRUSTING YOUR CHARACTER

Once a teen feels he has adequately recognized the adult's character, he makes a decision. If he feels the adult is safe enough to be vulnerable with, he will take a risk and trust that adult. If not, he'll back away.

Teens often test the waters with adults at this juncture. Even knowing that an adult is trustworthy, teens will still push the adults' buttons to test if the adult is sincere and strong enough to handle their feelings. Remember, teens who avail themselves to receive love from an adult feel vulnerable during this risky time, and this testing period serves as a way for him to back out.

If I make her mad enough, she'll see that I really am a jerk after all, he thinks. The cry of the teen's heart at this point is this: *Will you love me even though I am so frightened, so unlovable?*

If a parent passes the test in a teen's eyes, then he decides to trust the adult. He will express love and see what happens. If the parent recognizes these expressions and tenderly accepts them, the teen continues to trust. Often these cues are short and subtle. Failure for parents to recognize them can seem devastating to teens, but take heart— ignorance is more acceptable to teens than outright rejection—and most teens will persist. Overtures to love may feel sparse and infrequent, but they are important.

Teens learn to trust our receptivity and character slowly and cautiously. While their overtures of love indeed feel good though too infrequent, the teen delivers them not altruistically. He has yet another agenda—to prepare to receive love. As his exchange with the adult deepens, so does his sense of risk, provided that he tested adult character and found it safe, then trusted the adult to give love to ("She recognized my expression of love and liked it").

Now he makes a final decision, which feels the most important of all. *Will I allow myself to take her love?* If he chooses to risk taking this, he feels that the essence of who he is may change. This is very frightening for teens.

While adults cannot force their love onto their teens, it is crucial that they communicate love to them. Consistent communication of sincere love eventually breaks through to teens. The more he has been wounded (even by other adults), the longer he will take to receive love. But since his need to receive love is deep and real, eventually he will take it—provided he recognizes the safe character qualities and trustworthiness in the adult.

Chapter Six

VALUE OF THE SELF

U NDERSTANDING A TEEN'S NEED FOR A SENSE OF VALUE AS A
unique individual requires reaching beyond our own feelings as parents who cherish our children and recognize how
teens see themselves. Many parents are dumbfounded to discover how
poorly a teen feels about himself.

They wonder, *If we love and praise him so much, why does he have
such low self-esteem?* The reason for this can be explained by understanding a teen's very different perception of himself and his world.

Teens, being developmentally egocentric, believe that their
actions and thoughts are constantly on public display. They have an
imaginary audience that diligently critiques their every move, outfit,
and conversation. Teens decide to believe what "others" are thinking
about them, and their perceptions are filtered through opinions they
believe others hold about them. Thus, their feelings regarding their
identity and abilities are not always based in reality.

Needless to say, their opinions regarding themselves are quite
varied from their parents, who formulate opinions about their children from their more realistic sense of reality, rather than from perceptions of an imaginary audience. But while a parent esteems a

teen's identity and uniqueness, the teen may indeed see himself dramatically different.

A junior high principal recently asked me how he should deal with the "cliques" of girls surfacing in his school. He was concerned about snobbism taking hold, leading some girls to feel rejected. This prompted me to ask girls from each of the clusters why they wouldn't mix with one another.

There was a universal response from each side. "Oh, they wouldn't want to hang out with us," they said. "They don't like us."

"How do you know?"

"Oh, just look how they dress differently. We're sure they don't like us."

Clearly members of each group imagined what the other girls might say about them simply because they were experiencing an imaginary audience.

POSITIVE IMAGES

The word "esteem" means to raise up, to elevate. Healthy parenting involves teaching a process whereby a teen learns to recognize, embrace, and raise up the deepest truest sense of who he is. This is extremely important because the teen is then able to draw strength from that positive image of himself and move forward in life.

Erik Erikson outlined the stages of psychological development depicting tensions between two pathways at each stage. During the beginning stages of adolescence (ages eleven and twelve), we can see that as the identity emerges, the importance of liking, embracing, and valuing that identity is crucial. Erikson's stages of development are as follows:

Trust vs. mistrust (ages newborn to one year)
Autonomy vs. shame and doubt (ages one to two years)
Initiative vs. guilt (ages three to five)
Industry vs. inferiority (ages five to eleven)

Identity vs. role diffusion (ages eleven to twenty years)
Intimacy vs. isolation (ages twenty-one to forty)
Generativity vs. stagnation (ages forty to sixty)
Integrity vs. despair (ages sixty and older)[4]

According to Erikson, a teen stands at a painful juncture. As his identity is struggling to emerge, it is also threatened. For if his identity is not received and accepted, he will develop role diffusion. Role diffusion is the fragmentation of the self and the breakdown of identity in order to respond to those around him. If teens are allowed to mature in a healthy home, their identity will mature in a healthy fashion. Recognizing this powerful influence over teens can be a painful realization for parents who are experiencing a profound sense of isolation from them.

David Allen, writing in his book, *Shattering the Gods Within*, states, "The teenage years, with their many conflicts relating to sexuality, self-image, and dependency, places every young person under tremendous strain. Only in the environment of caring parents, peers, or significant others does the teenager develop a sense of identity as opposed to role diffusion or confusion."[5]

If, for example, the identity of a teen emerges amidst a parent who relies on him to meet his (the parent's) needs in an unhealthy fashion, the teen will respond accordingly. If his parent "needs" him to perform or behave in a certain manner, the teen's true self will retreat and his personal resources will meet that parent's needs. In essence, the parent drains him, thereby changing his personality in an unhealthy manner. The teen feels this (although he may not consciously recognize it), and in his frustration enters role diffusion.

Even teens who have suffered loss and confusion in the early years can be restored by parents during this time. My purpose is not to blame teens or parents but to restore healthy relationships between them. Many parents worry about the effects of their mistakes on kids, such as divorce, both parents working during the early years, and a multitude of other personal problems. Parents carry so much guilt that it threatens to paralyze or crush their motivation.

Be encouraged. Please remember that with teens it is never too late—and never too early. Adolescents are both children and young adults, and they will forever long for a mother or father to restore them.

Identity is part of a teen's sense of self-worth, including his perception of his uniqueness and his individuality. His identity, however, is given value because it is connected with another's identity.

Teens experience a frightening realization that they want to be independent and alone, but they are not. They are not to live disconnected from family or peers. In the midst of trying to separate, they realize that they are in fact interdependent, and this arouses another dimension in their thinking: *If I am supposed to be dependent, where do I fit in?*

Adlerian psychology teaches that humans need to experience a sense of belonging. We are part of a whole, and a teen's sense of value comes from being integrated into a larger unit—family, friends, and society. While each teen has individuality, he has a need to fit his uniqueness into a higher order. Naturally he learns this in the family structure. Family, after all, is the place of his most intense needs, dependency, and connectedness.

If he perceives that if he doesn't fit in, he becomes anxious, frustrated, and angry. When he does so, he often takes out his frustrations on his parents and siblings. Parents often take this anger personally, which can be a painful mistake.

Shirley Gould writes in her book, *Teenagers: The Continuing Challenge*, "The universal goal of all people is to be a value among other human beings . . . everyone craves satisfying relationships with others. The very survival of every person is dependent on interaction with others, from birth onward through life. That is the basis for the conflict among us. Everybody is constantly striving. Parents are striving for their own significance at the same time their children are striving to be independent." In the teen years the conflict between independence and connectedness intensifies. And this conflict occurs as their perception of self-worth evolves and matures.

Emergence of identity must occur for healthy development into adulthood. Equally important as emergence of identity is growth of self-esteem. Unfortunately, many of us adults (particularly women) never fully elevate our identity to the position originally intended. We, too, suffer from low self-esteem.

Emergence of the self involves development of the emotional, intellectual, physical, and spiritual aspects of who the teen is. Wonderfully, a teen begins to perceive this emergence and intuitively recognizes new depth in his being. He understands that he is physically more capable, emotionally more broad, and spiritually more deep. He is frightened to recognize the depth but excited to explore.

Parental interfacing at this juncture is as crucial to teens as standing behind the toddler when he proceeds with his first wobbly steps. He is tentative but doesn't know it. His fears express a desire for independence. Let us not be fooled.

Parental interfacing is important because healthy self-esteem for teens means instilling two crucial components: lovability and capability. For a teen to genuinely embrace a healthy sense of value, he must feel lovable and capable, all at the same time.

LOVABILITY

At the foundation of healthy character development for teens lies the fundamental need to feel lovable. This need is quite raw during adolescence, particularly since their world feels so tumultuous. There is a snag in the eyes of teens, however, because lovability embodies a sense of worthiness. When asked "Why do your parents love you?", many teens have responded to me with a litany of functions they have performed for their parents. Responses such as "because I don't give them much trouble" or "because I work hard in school" are heard a lot. I have never had a teen respond "they just love me because. . . ."

In a teen's mind his lovability to the most significant people in his life—his parents—is contingent upon his performance or behavior. And while we parents would like to assert otherwise, the truth is we tend to embrace our teens when they behave. Good kids are easier to love than tough kids. The problem is, however, that teens derive their sense of lovability from us, their parents.

Since they need to feel loved, they will either work hard for parents to feel "more worthy" of love, or they will rebel if they sense that they are unlovable to us. Thus, their natural instincts trap them either way, and parents recognizing what is going on can help release them from this dilemma.

Lovability, in fact, has nothing to do with worthiness. A teen needs to sense his own lovability simply because he is. Once he understands in the deepest part of himself that he is loved "just because," he will be free to develop sound decision-making skills and preserve his well-being.

In short, once a teen believes he is lovable, he becomes less vulnerable to a culture inviting him to feel more lovable by participating in its promises. Teens need to experience from parents that the essence of whom they are is good enough—good enough to deserve love. Jessica did not perceive herself to be worthy of love. Allison's fear of rejection and abandonment prompted her to fight like an alley cat. Michael enjoyed a very deep sense of lovability because his parents knew the importance of communicating this truth to their son.

Remember that there is a difference between parents loving their teen and a teenager's sense of lovability. Most parents would argue that their love is real, and indeed it is, but this doesn't mean that the teens feel lovable. From their perspective, they need to feel lovable. My purpose in outlining the needs of teens is to illustrate how parents can better meet those needs.

Modern psychology exposed the baby boomer generation to the notion that unconditional love was one of the deepest cravings of the human heart. *Aha!* we thought, *now we know what was missing in our lives.* Certainly we can learn from these voids and provide unconditional love to our children. This is a wonderful idea, but we are, in fact, poor lovers. We love better if our children behave and fail to communicate real love to those who need it most—our teen rebels.

The ideal unconditional lover is God Himself. He gives us a picture of perfect love to a world of messed-up adults. Many who have struggled with alcohol or drug addiction are privileged to understand this phenomenon of unconditional love. Adults bold enough to become spiritually intimate with God recognize their own need for lovability and can then transfer this into their relationships with teens.

CAPABILITY

Parental nurturing of teen capability comes quite naturally to most parents. We want our kids to be successful, to achieve, to show off their talents, particularly their physical talents. First, we identify what our kids are good at, then encourage them to pursue certain activities. Usually this amounts to identifying athletic talent and carting them to the nearest ball field, gym, or ice rink.

Fortunately, girls now have more athletic opportunities to identify their physical capabilities than in years past. While drawing out a teen's physical prowess is helpful in teaching capability, unfortunately there are two problems that tend to arise.

First, parents unwittingly confuse capability with lovability in the physical arena. Michael knew he was capable of running track well. He knew he was able to academically excel. While intellectual and physical capability is very important, caution must be issued. We parents can confuse meaningful lessons because of wrong motives.

Michael ran track, he told me, not so much for himself but for his parents. He felt on display, running perhaps as much to satiate confused parental desire as for his own understanding of his natural capabilities. Prompting our teens to compete because of our hidden motives restricts healthy lessons from being learned. What happens when teens "perform" for parents is that capability and lovability become entwined in the teen's perception, regardless of what the parents sincerely intend.

Second, when we elevate physical capability over emotional, intellectual, or spiritual capability, we leave teens feeling empty and frustrated. Truthfully, teens capable of enduring painful circumstances regarding loss in their lives (emotional capability) and savvy enough to negotiate through high school, college, and job interviews (intellectual capability) are better prepared for life than those displaying strong physical capabilities.

We parents, however, rarely encourage our kids to embrace their emotional capabilities in the way we do their physical attributes. It is tougher to teach kids to deal with sorrow than it is to coach soccer; to grieve the loss of a friend than to dance ballet; or to learn to resolve anger toward a grandparent than to take piano lessons. For teens, however, emotional and intellectual capabilities strengthen their self-esteem to a greater degree than their physical capabilities.

An idea that has all but dried up in our culture is teens' service to others. Before the Industrial Age, America's rural economy demanded that families work together as a unit, which meant that children and teens worked on the farm to enhance survival of everyone in the family. Older siblings tilled the soil, worked with the livestock, and cared for the younger ones. Even during World War II families under the strain of limited rations worked together to allot portions to individual family members.

In short, external pressures made each member of the family cognizant of the need to help another, which opened the door for family members to serve one another and feel needed. This forced self-centered teens to be "other-oriented" for moments during the day. In turn, this enhanced their understanding that they were emotionally and physically capable, which enhanced their self-esteem. Serving the family unit taught teens that they were capable of loving, capable of caring.

Spiritual capability refers to the capacity for a teen to know and love God. This describes the teen's willingness to reveal the deepest part of himself to God and allow God to direct him. Perhaps for teens this is less frightening than for adults. The beauty is, however, that any teen can embody this regardless of physical or intellectual limitations.

Spiritual knowledge in connection with God is an open invitation to any teen. I have known teens with Down's syndrome, grossly limited in physical and intellectual capacities, who have a sincere understanding of spiritual capability. I believe with all my heart that allowing God to infiltrate their spirit gives deep meaning and esteem to their lives. Understanding God's character and knowing His personality markedly enhances the teen's understanding of his own lovability from a God able to grant unconditional love.

Chapter Seven

SAFETY: PHYSICAL AND EMOTIONAL

I N A CULTURE REPLETE WITH INNER-CITY AND SUBURBAN GANGS, school shootings such as ones that we have witnessed in Littleton, Colorado, and Paducah, Kentucky, the need for safety would seem obvious, if not overwhelming.

Safety defined as an adolescent need refers not just to physical safety but to emotional safety as well. While we cannot provide either of these sufficiently outside of our homes, it is important that we model them within the immediate family structure. Let's look first at the need for physical safety.

PHYSICAL SAFETY

At birth we are born into a situation of complete dependency. Babies are dependent upon the care and love of a mother (most often) to insure their survival. Infants trust that provision for their physical needs will be made.

As children grow into toddlers, parents must bolster efforts to protect them from harm. Parents set up gates, cover up electric outlets, put away tiny objects that could be swallowed, and create special areas in which toddlers can roam without harming themselves. Adults impose boundaries for the toddler because he has no sense of danger or consequences for his actions. His perceptions are distorted because of his cognitive limitations. Therefore, loving parents do their best to preserve and keep him safe.

Teenagers, believe it or not, are much like toddlers. Their cognitive limitations prevent them from appreciating future consequences resulting from an action today. The inability to think abstractly or connect future consequences with present actions—coupled with the embodiment of the "personal fable"—sets them at tremendous health risks.

What is the "personal fable"? The personal fable is the belief that they are unlike any other in their vulnerability to a life-threatening danger. Indeed, they believe that they will never get seriously hurt, contract a serious illness, become pregnant, or die.

Teens are like two people wrapped into one: half child, half adult. Their adult-sized bodies fool us, leading us to believe that their understanding of danger may be as mature as their speech, dress, or athletic ability. But we must not be fooled.

Teens need physical protection, but logistics pose a problem. They are out of our sight most of the day, and toddler gates and electric outlet covers just won't do. But we must continue to put forth diplomatic efforts toward insuring as much physical safety as possible. Let's look at why this is important.

When we restrain toddlers with gates and car seats, they can be expected to experience frustration, but when teens see parents exerting efforts at making certain they wear seat belts, come home by 11 p.m. and stay away from junk food, their perception of their own worth increases, whether you believe it or not. While they can be expected to resist parental concern outwardly, internally they are defining their physical worth. *If Mom and Dad show concern for my well-being, my health and my body must be important to them. I'm valuable to them.*

As this thinking is reinforced through the adolescent years, quite naturally the teen-turning-adult will assume the role of protecting himself. Hence, he internalizes his parents' beliefs about protecting his body and mind. This internalization process affords him the ability to keep himself safer while elevating his self-esteem at the same time. This helps him establish healthy boundaries and have a deeper sense of sanctity with respect to his body—which is extremely important when he comes to make decisions about his sexual activity.

The healthy teen emerges from adolescence with a new sense that his body is defined, is to be revered, deserves protection, and is valuable. These messages are integrated into the adult psyche through repeated modeling of protection of the physical self by the people with the greatest authority in his life—Mom or Dad.

Logistically, we wonder how we can accomplish this without acting as military sergeants. First, this modeling, as alluded to earlier, must begin during the early years, but this is not always possible if you are a stepparent or a grandparent assuming care of the teen at the onset of adolescence.

Remember first that teens are mimickers. They watch, listen, wait, test, and wait some more before deciding how they will behave. Therefore, example, care, and preservation of yourself is very important.

A JARRING INCIDENT

I remember an incident two years ago when I was jogging. A couple of miles into my run a car with two men in their twenties pulled up beside me. One leaned out his window and began asking me several inappropriate questions. Although I ignored them, they continued to follow and harass me. I bolted into a nearby store, ran out the back, and darted home. Never again would I run at dusk alone.

My daughters weren't interested in jogging at the time, and I remember wondering whether or not I should share the incident with them. I didn't want to frighten them, but I wanted them to be wise. In the end, I decided to share the harrowing incident with them, and they were frightened. I reminded them we are not to be fearful but to act wisely.

Acting wisely applies to the confusing messages our culture gives adolescents regarding the value of their bodies. Many Hollywood movies, television advertisements, magazine covers, etc., prod teens into believing there should be few, if any, boundaries to their bodies. This can be devastating to their self-esteem and encourages teen boys to treat their bodies as an appendage to fleeting emotions. The message distilled: do anything you like, no problem.

But there *is* a problem for boys and for girls. Intuitively, they long for boundaries, for adult validation to protect and to preserve a huge part of themselves that makes them feel valued and loved. Parents *must* communicate to teens that their bodies are sacred and worth protecting. Teens long for adults to set limits to insure that they are not placed in a situation where they are vulnerable or overpowered.

Lisa came to see me when she was twelve. She was physically quite beautiful and had a very tender spirit. She was the oldest of three siblings, and her parents were proud of her as she entered high school. At fourteen she did well scholastically and excelled at piano.

Apparently, many upperclassmen appreciated her gifts, and one young fellow in particular pursued her, although her parents were adamant in not allowing her to date until she was fifteen. Ted waited patiently until she reached that magic age to ask her out. Mom and Dad balked at first because Ted was almost eighteen, but they liked his personality and let Lisa date him regularly on weekends.

Lisa was enamored with Ted when their dating began. In her eyes he was mature (he was a senior), powerful (soccer captain and star), and handsome. Having Ted as her boyfriend made Lisa feel better about her worth as a person. He was her adornment, her prize. And sadly, on some level her parents felt stroked because their sophomore daughter was dating the captain of the soccer team.

Within six months of dating, Lisa became pregnant. Lisa carried the baby, gave her up for adoption, and was fortunate enough to have support for her decision in the midst of a painful time from her family. Ted didn't abandon her, but after the baby was born, they split up. Lisa is emotionally stable now—and more mature.

Physical safety: what went wrong for Lisa? While Lisa's parents couldn't be there during their dates, they should have recognized that Lisa was out of her league dating a boy two-and-a-half years older. Physically, she was overpowered, and she was certainly at a disadvantage emotionally and intellectually as well. She looked up to him, believing him to be more sophisticated.

Time after time young girls enter relationships where they're not on equal ground with boys they date. The same is true for young adolescent males, though this scenario is less common. Parents do their teens a disservice by failing to protect them from vulnerable situations in which they can be emotionally manipulated, physically overpowered, or psychologically disadvantaged.

Allison enjoyed no sense of protection in her home. Mom and her stepdad were alcoholics, and many nights it was Allison who checked the locks on the doors before she went to bed. But the greatest insult came to Allison when she was sexually assaulted at nine years of age by her stepdad. Months went by before she told her mother, who refused to believe her. Not only did her mother fail to protect her, she assisted her in feeling crazy, guilty, and deeply shameful. That should not happen.

EMOTIONAL SAFETY

Emotional safety may appear to be a confusing concept, but it is quite straightforward. That progression is as follows: First, teens respond to a situation and specific feelings are evoked: anger, hurt, rejection, etc.

Somewhere in this process, if healthy emotional patterns are followed, emotions must be externalized through discussion (particularly if they are potent emotions). If they are received and directed by parents or other significant adults, resolution occurs and specific feelings are left behind. Emotionally the event will pass and its impact diffused.

If this process of feelings, externalization of these feelings, followed by resolution is interrupted, serious results can occur. Teens, for instance, involved with inner-city gangs harbor deep feelings of anger that have never been nurtured to resolution by wiser adults or peers. The result is an outward explosion of snowballing rage, which often controls their thinking and their actions. Hence, the rise of gang-related crime.

Emotional safety occurs on two different levels. First, an emotionally safe environment is one in which, as author and lecturer John Bradshaw describes, *"A child may be given the freedom to feel what he feels and see what he sees."* This is the opportunity for feelings to be recognized and received in order that emotions may resolve in a healthy manner. Parents cannot dictate how adolescents feel. We would like to at times, but we can't. We can help them, however, grow into emotionally healthy young adults if we can accept and validate their feelings.

Mary brought Dan in for his fifteen-year-old physical. Usually teen boys prefer having my husband, also a physician, do the exam, but he was unavailable. Thus, Dan was stuck with me. I sensed at the beginning of the appointment that he was anxious.

"Good morning, Dan," I started, trying to put him at ease. "How are you doing?"

"All right," he complied.

"I just want to let you know that I'm glad to catch up with you. I know you usually see my husband, so if there is anything you would rather discuss with him, that's no problem. We'll just schedule a later visit with him."

Dan's face expressed thanks, and he relaxed as I laid before him a safety net. He understood that while I needed to perform the physical exam, I respected his desire for privacy and his discomfort with me.

His mother jumped into the conversation. "Dr. Meeker, I've gotta be honest with you," she began. "I don't know if Dan will tell you this, so I will. School is going terribly. He hates his teachers and fights with one kid in particular. I don't know what to do."

"Dan, what's going on at school?" I looked at him.

"It stinks," his head dropped, looking away from me.

"Can you tell me what stinks at school?" I asked.

Dan discoursed for a full ten minutes about his dislikes regarding school, the kids, the courses, a teacher named Mr. Symons, lunch break, even PE. His mother interrupted frequently, and I repeatedly asked her to let Dan finish. He did, but his frustration was broad.

When the time came for me to examine Dan, I asked Mary to leave the room.

"Dan, what makes you say Mr. Symons is a jerk?"

"Oh, brother. Every time he asks me a question, he never lets me raise my hand, he just asks. I never know the answer. I feel like such an idiot."

I listened to his chest, then pulled the stethoscope from my ears.

"Dan, that would make me feel pretty uncomfortable. How about you?"

"Yeah, I hate it. He makes me feel really stupid. He's just a jerk." Dan was becoming more comfortable.

"Can you talk to your mom or dad about Mr. Symons?" I asked.

"Yeah, at first I did. I told them I wanted to switch classes, and they said just to wait it out. I told my parents what an idiot he was, but they didn't believe me. They just defended him and said I wasn't allowed to call him names—it was disrespectful. Whenever I try to talk to my mom, she tells me to stop talking like that. Dad, well, he just gets really mad, so I don't talk to him."

Dan and his parents were caught in a typical pattern of communication entanglement. Dan's problem, I learned, wasn't with school or with students or even lunch period. Dan's problem was with interaction with his teacher. Mr. Symons's style of teaching evoked feelings of humiliation in Dan. Whenever he called on him, Dan felt stupid and ashamed.

At home, Mary and her husband received Dan's frustration and witnessed him behave with disrespect and angry outbursts. Mary took his feelings personally (believing his anger was toward her, not his teacher) and rather than standing back, listening, and dissecting his feelings, she simply stated, "You're not allowed to call your teacher names." Dan interpreted this statement as an assault on his feelings. Internally he heard, *You're not allowed to feel this way toward any of your teachers or your school.*

This added to his frustration, and his school performance worsened. His dad's response was fairly typical for an exhausted father. He reacted to Dan's frustration with greater frustration—sometimes yelling—and Dan's original feelings of humiliation from Mr. Symons were further invalidated. Home was not a place of emotional safety for Dan because the feelings he had were not received or validated.

Mary and her husband were good parents, and when I talked to them about validating Dan's feelings, they made an effort to do just that. They initiated a few changes in communication, which made life much more pleasant. Dan's attitude toward school dramatically improved. What he needed was an environment where he could identify what he felt, be aided in identifying the root of those feelings, and then be guided as to what to do with those feelings. Mary became quite good at helping him.

Why is meeting this need crucial to healthy teen development? Because it allows teens to formulate healthy and accurate perceptions of their environment. Dan, for example, experienced genuine humiliation when he couldn't answer questions in Mr. Symons's class.

Humiliation is devastating to a fifteen-year-old boy beginning to shave facial hair but still wanting the comfort of his mother.

When his parents initially responded to his humiliation with messages that he wasn't to feel that way, he began to believe that he wasn't sizing things up quite right. Something was wrong with *him*. When parents communicate to teens that their feelings are wrong (and we often do this without thinking), teens begin to doubt the accuracy of their perceptions. Teens are not yet mature enough to realize that they may be sizing up the situation more accurately than they think. Thus, they experience self-doubt and greater confusion. Parents who recognize this dynamic are doing something very crucial to healthy emotional development.

The second component of an emotionally safe environment involves a place, a time, and an opportunity for teens to express feelings and have them accepted. These suggestions sometimes raise hairs on posterior spines of most parents who feel, *There is no way I am going to let my teenager rant and rave around my house. He already does that, and we're both miserable.*

This second element of emotional safety involves healthy patterns of emotional expression. Meeting this need, in fact, can be accomplished by clear guidelines set by parents who are teaching teens how to deal with and express themselves, but often it is uncontrolled, unfocused, and destructive. Healthy expression—or externalization of feelings—requires direction and gentle teaching, which must be done in an environment of acceptance, receptivity, authority, and concern.

Many emotional tangles parents have with teens are so frustrating and painful that parents often give up. Providing emotional safety in a home doesn't require a psychology degree: it just takes one willing parent.

Physical safety, providing protection for the physical self and for basic physical needs, invests a sense that they are worth caring for and worth loving. Emotional safety teaches teens to accurately recognize their feelings and their perceptions of the environment around them. We must allow teens to resolve their feelings and finally to make healthy decisions regarding whether or not they should act upon what they are feeling inside.

Many teens, however, never resolve their feelings, which end up snowballing on top of one another, leaving them confused and feeling out of control. Real control, however, stems from an ability to identify feelings and make decisions regarding them.

I identify these forms of safety as needs because unless they are met, teens are lost. Over the years that I have been treating teens, I have sadly seen a rise in the number of lost and broken teens walking through my exam room doors. Restoration of these lost souls requires going back to the basics, underlining the most fundamental of needs, and reeducating ourselves about how we can best meet them.

Chapter Eight

TENDER HEARTS
IN A TOUGH CULTURE

HISTORICALLY, FAMILIES HAVE BEEN THE PRIMARY INFLUENCES upon children's character development. Parents instill values in their children by spending time with them, working with them, talking with them. Good lessons and bad lessons are learned within the family structure, with Mom or Dad passing along their wisdom.

With economics mobilizing mothers into the work force and fathers spending more time away from home, communication time with teens has become fragmented. More than any time in history, teens are home alone during afternoons—the most vulnerable time for delinquent activity.

The result? Today's culture plays a heightened influence in shaping teen character—and parents are relegated to a lessened influence. This phenomenon is a direct result of decreased time that parents spend with their teens.

Recognizing the four fundamental teen needs of love, value, intimacy, and safety, consider the opportunity that teens take to have these needs met outside of the family unit. Movies, television programs, music, athletics, and peers are just a few of the ways that our culture reaches our teens. The vacuum has occurred because the family unit, in too many cases, is no longer available to meet their needs.

In 1990, medical researchers Brown, et. al. showed that parental absence was associated with an increased use of TV and radio by adolescents.[6] Let us consider some of the cultural changes teens contend with on a daily basis and how these influences affect their fundamental needs.

MEDIA, MUSIC, AND MTV

Some studies cite that the average teen watches between twenty to twenty-three hours per week of television—an average of three hours per day.[7] Dr. Victor Strasburger in his paper, "Children, Adolescents and Television," discusses what an average American youngster will be exposed to during his lifetime. Strasburger cites these findings: young people will hear more than 14,000 sexual references, innuendoes and jokes; view more than 1,000 murders, rapes, assaults, and armed robberies; and be blitzed by 20,000 commercials during their lifetime.[8]

Nationally known sociologist and speaker Tony Campolo pinpoints the 1977 movie *Star Wars* as the major turning point in opening the floodgate of media influence in the lives of teens and younger children. *Star Wars'* usage of other-world images and a futuristic plot captivated a generation of youngsters.

Television, computers, video games, and virtual reality are the *new* reality. "One reason adults may underestimate this medium is because they know television is fantasy," writes Strasburger. "However, children lack adult reasoning abilities and often view the television world as being realistic and shape their behaviors accordingly."[9]

MUSIC IN THE LIVES OF TEENS

Music has historically been a mirror of the culture, calling teens into an unfamiliar but safe world. At a time when teens long to dissect their world and feelings, music comes along and contrasts those feelings with their mom's or dad's. Songs have proven to be havens of safety to adolescents, who can voyeuristically participate through listening. The fantasy of musical life is a powerful draw—so powerful, in fact, that teens spend hour upon hour listening to their favorite music.

Do teens listen to music in their rooms just to frustrate their parents, making a statement regarding the uniqueness of their taste in music? Answer: teens allow—even invite—music to replace their immediate world of feelings and frustrations with another. Songs provide an emotional safety net for teens' feelings to be validated. Popular music never rejects the listener.

Now consider MTV and movies. Combine the potency of music with visual imagery and the seduction becomes more than they can resist—or at least want to resist. Visual and auditory stimuli tap like a hot iron into all of the senses, save touch and smell. Emotionally torn teenagers, physically feeling as though their bodies hang between childhood and adulthood, remain entirely vulnerable to the titillations of the screen. Their days are around-the-clock sessions of sorting life out, and their defenses are ripe for influence because teens are not even sure if they should have defenses; even they are controversial in the adolescent psyche.

Unquestionably, television does affect teen behavior. *The National Institute for Mental Health Summary Report released in 1982 showed that violence on television does lead to violence in youth.*[10] In addition, numerous surveys found that exposure to sexually suggestive materials, especially MTV and R-rated films, is "significantly associated with premarital sexual promiscuity among youth."[11]

Considering the fundamental needs depicted in the previous chapter, let's examine why media, music, and audio-visual games have such spellbinding effects on teens. In fact, their enticeability makes a lot of sense. The problem with these art forms is that they do not represent reality.

Virtual reality infused into the tender adolescent mind can be devastating because it occurs at a developmental stage when kids are deciphering truth from non-truth. One of the primary goals of parenting is to help our teens mature to a state where they can grasp a sense of what they can influence and what aspects of life they can't. Teaching the emerging self to sift through life experiences on a variety of levels and reach a truthful conclusion is integral in the development of healthy adults. Media, music, and movies can, if not wisely monitored, scramble their ability to live in an authentic reality.

MEDIA: INTIMACY AND SAFETY

Tony Campolo describes the lure of movies to teens as an intimacy issue. Reflecting on intimacy as a need for teens and all human beings to connect with one another, it is quite natural for teens to gravitate toward the silver screen. Films have unique ways of introducing emotions in which actors and actresses cry out, "Someone take me, someone look at me."

Teens are drawn to these characters on the screen. They are free to respond, and they have a need to respond since the stories and music move them. Teens believe—or try hard to believe—that they are there. They want intimacy, connection, and an exchange of responsiveness with the man or woman on the screen, but it is fake, and they have no one to tell them so. They have a genuine cry of their souls for intimacy, but the problem is that they are too introspective to stand back and see what's going on. So they try again, perhaps popping in another movie, cranking up the headset, or watching a new music video.

What about their need for safety? It's "filled" there as well. We know they need a time and a place to feel, or better yet to have an outside source (person) help direct their deep feelings. Media, quite naturally, plays a serious role in evoking feelings from teenagers with hearts in hiding. Violent movies prick their sense of mastery and domination, and in front of the screen, they can fantasize all they want without anyone seeing them. Every imaginable emotion can be tapped into, and even the emotions they don't want to feel. This is particularly true for teen boys.

Teen girls are no less of a target. Perhaps verbose tendencies allow them to feel and express feelings more safely than teen boys, but there is still titillation wrought from the screen and CDs. Teen girls, too, enjoy the safety of feeling fear, horror, and pangs of love.

Extrusion of any feeling is possible with a flick of a switch. And again this pertains even to the emotions they'd rather not feel. Many music videos depict overt allusions to sexual violence against young girls, but girls continue to watch. Why? Because experience of emotion—even crude emotions of self-contempt—allures the psyche in progress. Teens haven't yet developed decisions regarding who they are, or if they indeed like who they are. Therefore, even feelings of self-contempt are up for grabs.

In summation, media for teenagers provides intimacy, or at least some superficial form of it.

MEDIA AND SELF-ESTEEM

Recognizing the potent push-and-pull of various media forms on the pliable psyches of teens, consider its effect on the emergence of teen identity. The basic need of hearts of all ages is the need to feel valued. The teenage years are the time when this uniqueness emerges, but it is a paradox: as their desire for individuality and definition surfaces, fear abounds.

That fear revolves around the need for acceptance: "If people see that I am different, will they accept me?" Since teens fear rejection, they conform to various expectations of their peer group in order to find acceptance. Herein lies the paradox: *I need to have uniqueness, but I want to be like you.* The inner self searches for value and a deeper sense of worth, but the outer conformity stems from fear of rejection.

Admittedly, emotions are churning below the surface. Adult desires and adult thinking patterns are making the teen uncomfortable. These patterns are restructuring the teen's sense of who he is, who he will become. This reorganization makes him uncomfortable, so he reverts back to the way he has always been—dependent and childlike. Since that is not possible, he is terrified that no one will like the "new" him, so he conforms because there is safety in being like everyone else.

When MTV, music, and other media present themselves to teens who are reorganizing internally and conforming externally, they find an audience primed for influence. Since teens fear rejection, they gravitate toward the safest source, such as the TV. Shows, sitcoms, and movies of the week have on display the sexually promiscuous, the violent, the social outcasts, the class cut-ups. Teens wonder (usually subconsciously) which ones they are most like.

These figures are attractive because strands deep within them find commonality with these people. Teens can pretend to be a little of each. What feels right, they can keep; what doesn't, they can discard. A male teen, for example, feels comfortable in identifying with the sexually promiscuous, the comic, or the dominant male in control of his world, but then he can make a dangerous leap in his mind: *If I feel like them, I can become like them.*

Here the conforming power takes hold of him internally, and he becomes like the character on the screen. He is a chameleon, creating a false self-identity based on images from a screen. Sometimes this conformity is temporary, sometimes it is not. Either way, he surrenders his true self for a time.

This mimicry has been documented. In 1992, Strasburger wrote that "children learn by imitating adults. According to Bandura's social learning theory, children learn new behaviors by observing others, directly in real life and vicariously through the media, and they are more likely to imitate a behavior if they see an adult rewarded for it. Such modeling is a key element in television's effects."[12]

There is another reason why conformity to media characters is powerful in the lives of teens: glamour. Glamour presents media celebrities as larger than life. To the adolescent mind, if a celebrity is admired by the culture, then the teen allows that media celebrity into his own life. In the teen's mind, it is okay for him to continue feeling these feelings (sexual, violent, etc.) and act on them. The television personality has succeeded in influencing the teen to conform.

Glamour—which cloaks television or music celebrities with authority—entices teens to perpetuate chameleon behavior: *Here, take it; try it.* And there is another benefit—friends agree. Since subcultures of teens tend to admire common media personalities, they find acceptance from friends as they adopt and admire the latest celebrity. Glamour begets authority. Authority begets conformity. And conformity begets acceptance. *Finally,* the teen rationalizes, *if I am accepted, then I am worth something.*

But what about the true self in the real world of the teens? Is there hope in the midst of media influences? Absolutely, and as we will see later, parents play a crucial role in this. Parents provide strength, acceptance, and guidance to the teens' character. Reality is less glamorous, and parents are infinitely more boring than media figures. But be assured that beneath the desire for superficial acceptance is the genuine need to experience lovability and capability taught by parents. The need to experience these attributes from parents is deeper and more powerful in teens, and it outweighs media influence.

There's another influence that has to be dealt with, and that's in the sexual arena, as we'll see in the next chapter.

Chapter Nine

THE SEXUAL REVOLUTION: ITS EFFECT ON PARENTS AND THEIR TEENS

Lo! With a little rod
I did but touch the honey of romance—
And must I lose a soul's inheritance?

OSCAR WILDE

IT IS MY CONVICTION THAT OUR POST-SEXUAL REVOLUTION CUL-
ture impacts the emerging sexuality of teens more potently than
any other part of their character. The consequences of its influences can be damaging and even life-threatening. For this reason I will
now focus on the influence of a teen's immediate culture on his sexuality and his sexual behavior.

Baby boomer parents, including myself, have a problem on our
hands. Our upbringing was penetrated with the breakdown of sexual
barriers and inhibitions. The sexual revolution surfacing in the sixties

gained steam in the seventies, influencing the American mindset to accept freedom in sexual relationships—freedom to engage in sexual promiscuity and experience a variety of sexual relationships outside of marriage. If we didn't embrace sexual freedom in our lives, at least we learned tolerance and acceptance in our friends' lives. Sexual freedom became the norm for the baby boomer generation, much to the distress of our parents.

It's just been in the last ten or fifteen years that we are learning that no freedom exists without a cost. The cost has been escalating teen pregnancy rates, cervical cancer in teens rather than in older women, a multitude of horrific sexually transmitted diseases, and HIV seeping beyond the borders of the homosexual and hemophiliac communities.

Regardless of statistical risks for these diseases, parents are scared for their teens. Parents partially bought into "safe sex" teaching until their intuitions proved correct and enormous holes were detected in the theory. Now we're even more frightened. We knew safe sex didn't make much sense, but now what do we do?

For the first time in American history, parents are faced with the difficulty of teaching their teens that they (the teens) cannot embrace a freedom that their parents had. We have to reverse a liberty for the safety of the kids, which evokes indecision and guilt in the minds of parents.

Baby boomer parents who believe that sexual freedom was beneficial—even acceptable—need these theories of "safe sex" to work. We need them to be reasonable because it keeps us off the hook. If we could find a way to preserve a freedom "enjoyed" by our generation, then we wouldn't have to (1) admit that what we had was wrong (at least harmful), or (2) struggle with urging our teens not to do something that we did.

That's why baby boomer parents are often indecisive regarding our teens' sexual activity. We are frightened for what could happen to them, but we don't feel we have the tools to instruct and teach them. We feel helpless because being sexually active has taken center stage in teen culture. Baby boomer parents find themselves saying to themselves, "I had it, but they can't," leading them to do nothing.

This allows cultural permissiveness to seep into our homes. We feel impotent in a culture screaming "Yes, you can have it all, including sexual freedom." Our teens are lured by magazine features, television shows, and music lyrics celebrating sexual activity. Our teen culture has been oversexualized, and sex is used to sell everything from pick-up trucks to beer. Ads containing sexual innuendo increase sales and market share.

Teens are targeted because they are open, vulnerable, and undecided regarding sexual activity. They haven't yet lived through sexually transmitted diseases, infertility, and possibly HIV; they think they are invincible. But baby boomer parents can no longer remain standing on the sidelines feeling guilty.

The sad thing is that all this sexual talk should not occupy center stage in their lives—at least not yet. Even for baby boomers immersed in the sexual revolution, decisions regarding sexual involvement were not central issues—they were appendages to the rest of life's concerns. This has been a grave reversal, but we must acknowledge its position and power in order to set things right for our teens.

It is interesting that we endorse anti-smoking campaigns, anti-drug campaigns, and anti-drinking campaigns in teens. While these are all worthwhile, the truth is that no campaign to date is as universally fatal as HIV in the bloodstream.

We never advertise a safe way for teens to smoke or take drugs. We exhort teens *not* to engage in activities that could kill them, but when it comes to sexual activity, I don't believe we are as convinced about the dangers; although, as we will see in the ensuing chapters, we should be.

After all, we survived the Sexual Revolution and so will the next

generation. That thinking is not correct, and indeed the next generation is in markedly grave danger.

SCHOOL-BASED SEX EDUCATION PROGRAMS

You may be wondering why I am including school-based sex education programs in our discussion of major cultural influences on teens.
I believe that this is important because sex ed programs seriously contribute to the confusion our teens experience regarding their future
sexual behavior.

Let me be clear at the outset: education and frank discussion with
our teens is extremely important, and a premise of this book is that we
parents aren't doing enough of it. Many parents opposed to sex education programs have expressed concern about the subject of sexual
activity being broached. Their concern is usually twofold: the first one
being that increasing discussion will increase sexual involvement. My
experience has been, and I am not alone, that this is not true.

The other concern of some parents is that the sex ed classroom
discussions will be devoid of character-building information, leaving
teens and pre-adolescents with the view that sexual activity is nothing
more unique than eating breakfast and getting dressed in the morning. Thus, teens may feel inappropriately secure in trying sex out.

My clinical experience and research on school-based sex ed programs indicates that this is true, though not universally. From my position as a physician, sexuality and sexual activity teaching must be
approached, but I believe with a more positive, affirming message that
bolsters teens as capable of postponing that activity.

Maturing sexuality and increased focus on sexuality through
media, peers, and school programs casts it as a powerful influence in
the lives of teens.

Statistics in the medical literature regarding teen sexual activity are
alarming. Hayes cites in *Risking the Future: Adolescent Sexuality,
Pregnancy and Child-Bearing*, that "over 40 percent of women in the

United States will become pregnant before they reach the age of twenty."[13] In addition to the large social concerns and physical problems of the teen and child, there can be painful psychological problems associated with pregnancy.

Again, medical research from Kirby, et al, states, "Unfortunately, there can also be many negative consequences of adolescent sexual behavior. Some of them, such as feelings of exploitation, dissatisfaction, and guilt, are not easily quantified."[14]

Our culture at large agrees that something must be done to help teens live healthier lives, which most agree means reducing sexual activity. When professionals discuss how extensively teen sexual activity must be reduced, controversy erupts. Parents disagree, teachers disagree, feminists disagree, but most physicians who are up to date regarding the physical health risks disagree very little. I have never met a physician in adolescent or gynecological medicine who could, in all good conscience, state that teens who engage in sexual activity is medically acceptable or healthy. To encourage teens to be sexually active verges on malpractice.

People with different worldviews read the facts differently, which is why we continue to have broad disagreement about how to keep our kids sexually "safe." Many parents have thrust the responsibility primarily in the laps of public schools.

A review of school-based programs illustrates that most include teaching on abstinence, condom use, contraceptive use, and what sexually transmitted diseases and HIV are. The effectiveness of these programs? Not very impressive. In 1994, the Centers for Disease Control and Prevention commissioned a team of researchers to review twenty-three school-based programs that had been published in professional journals. Their conclusions?

"Not all sex- and AIDS-education programs had significant effects on adolescent sexual risk-taking behavior, but specific programs did delay the initiation of intercourse, reduce the frequency of intercourse, reduce the number of sexual partners, and increase the use of condoms or other contraceptives."[15]

Obviously, delaying onset of intercourse doesn't keep teens from getting sexually transmitted diseases, but it may help reduce cervical dysplasias. Increasing use of condoms may reduce pregnancies, but they don't necessarily make sex more safe. The Medical Institute was founded by Dr. Joe McIlhaney, a skilled obstetrician/gynecologist who was tired of treating infertility—much of it related to sexually transmitted diseases. He was discouraged to diagnose cervical cancers in younger and younger women, a direct result of intercourse at an early age.

Dr. McIlhaney decided to research the best medical literature available on sexually transmitted diseases, teen pregnancy rates, and the efficacy of school-based sex ed programs. Then he committed to present medical data to the general public. His review of excellent medical data shows that school-based programs aren't affecting teens in a positive way. Teens continue to be as sexually active as ever, and they continue to be influenced by a culture that tells them to go ahead and do it anyway—just "be safe."

Teachers of well-intended sex education programs know this frustration. Parents are scared, and kids are getting pregnant. Is this the way things are supposed to work?

Let's put all these influences together and view them from a teen's perspective. Teens watch at least twenty hours per week of television, which beams into their tender psyche a litany of sexual references and innuendo. They make decisions about sexual activity without much discussion from parents (one-fourth of parents talk to their kids about sex).[16]

Those parents who do engage teens probably grew up in the Sexual Revolution, and are thus confused about what to tell their kids. Then teens go to school and receive teaching heavily weighted on contraceptives rather than restraint. Result: their sexuality is up for grabs. Fears about sexual activity loom in their minds while they hear voices in songs or sitcoms urging them to try sex out. These kids are confused and need our help.

The Sexual Revolution carved out a generation of parents ill-equipped to handle their teen's sexual pressures. Media and the culture succeeded in seducing teens to believe that whether or not to have sex was their decision—and no one else's. This serves to confuse the budding sexuality of teens.

I believe with all my heart that this confusion surrounding sexual activity is at the heart of the trouble facing our teens. Teens intuitively know that their sexuality is important and has value. When those teens are immersed in a culture that assaults them with continual sexual messages, teens become tormented. They perceive that their sexuality is being manipulated by the media and poorly directed by physicians, confused parents, and exhausted teachers. The result is that they act upon their sexual urges and dig themselves into very deep holes.

Why is attendance to our teens' sexuality so important? Because sexuality is intertwined to their emotions, psychological maturity, physical health, and spirituality. When sexuality is confused, then all aspects of teen identity are confused as well. At the heart of restoring the teenage soul, therefore, is the restoration of teen sexuality. Teens can't do it alone—they need adult help.

Let's turn for a moment and view life from a teen's perspective, living with a barrage of sexual messages and indecisive adult counsel. Music and media, school-based sex education programs, and parental input all enter the minds of our adolescents at some stage, as we'll see in the next chapter.

Chapter Ten

THREE TOXIC MESSAGES

SOME OF THE DEEPEST DAMAGE DONE TO TEENS IN OUR CULTURE is done to their maturing sexuality. The combined social influences cited in the last chapter pack three toxic messages, pointed particularly at teen boys. Let's look at each message in detail in order to understand how we adults can help.

1. Your sexuality is so powerful that you are not expected to keep it under your control.

Successful advertisers promote their products using sexual references because they know it increases sales. Many recognize adolescents as the most easily influenced cultural subgroup, so advertisers target teens with their products, laced with sexual themes. The very premise upon which advertisers operate is that teens are expected to act upon their sexual urges.

Why make an issue out of this? Because teens are barraged with sexually charged advertisements on a regular basis. And with each ad, damage occurs: not only in the overt sexual suggestion, but also in the communication of adult expectations regarding teen behavior. Advertisers are not alone in operating upon these assumptions regarding teen behavior; the medical community is responsible as well.

I was recently discussing the problem of adolescent sexually transmitted diseases (STDs) with an obstetrician-gynecologist colleague. His tone as we discussed treatment for these teens was one of frustration. He felt overwhelmed with trying to arrest these illnesses even in our small number of shared patients. In short, practicing medicine amongst teens left him with the assumption that teens will be sexually active.

My colleague's expectations echo those of the medical community at large. Public schools approach sex education with the same foundational assumption—teens will be sexually active, so treatment should center on damage control. Have you any doubts? Look at many high school curriculums. Most are more heavily weighted on contraception (*you will be sexually active*) than on abstinence (*you have the ability to choose*).

Why is this important? There are two reasons. First, underlying adult expectations of teen behavior can dramatically affect teen behavior. From teens' perspective, if the medical and educational communities believe that they will be sexually active (even just to "try it out"), sexual activity is a done deal. Second, if no one around them operates on the assumption that they have a choice, their sense of control over their bodies has been lost. This perceived loss of control can have devastating psychological and developmental consequences.

The teen years are a critical time when teens learn healthy separation from parents. This occurs on physical, intellectual, and emotional levels as teens learn to recognize their own capabilities. They take responsibility for certain actions and the consequences regarding themselves. This choice, or control, is central to healthy teen separation. Learning control over oneself and accepting responsibility for one's behavior is the very foundation for healthy psychological maturity into adulthood.

Teens living in today's culture perceive that their sexuality is beyond their control. It is not. And parents must teach teens where the real power lies: in their intellectual and emotional dimensions. Adults must communicate to teens that we expect them to be able to draw upon their intellectual and emotional strengths to make sound choices about their sexual behaviors and furthermore, that we will help them do so.

2. Your sexuality is larger than other dimensions of who you are.

No healthy parent would endorse this statement. As my husband, Walt, and I glance at our teenage daughter across the dinner table, we revel in her tenderness toward her hurting friends and steam over her stubbornness. She is lovable to us because we have tangled and loved deeply together for many years. When we reflect on what makes her wonderful to us, ranking her thoughts, feelings, and athletic abilities, her sexuality enters at the bottom of the list. But this is in the mind of a parent. What we see regarding our teen's significance is very different from what she sees.

Let's look at life from Eric's perspective for a moment, in order to understand why he might see that his sexuality is larger than his athletic or intellectual abilities.

Eric is a boy of sixteen whose sex ed class is right after calculus. In sex ed, he learns about abstinence, sexually transmitted diseases, how to reduce risk of pregnancy, and how not to contract a potentially fatal illness such as HIV. Afterward, he has basketball practice for two hours and returns to the locker room. While showering, he hears a couple of seniors commenting on the beautiful figure of a classmate. He listens but doesn't say anything. Then Eric refocuses his train of thought onto his homework that night.

He drives home from school and spots a billboard of a motorboat draped by a scantily clad, busty woman. She is enormous, larger than life. Seeing her image confirms in his mind that he is sexually charged by the female form.

He arrives home to an empty house since Mom and Dad work.

Eric decides to relax for an hour in front of the TV. He flips the channel to MTV and settles on a few music videos. Guess what they're singing about? Loneliness, love, and lust.

Let's imagine that Eric is a "good kid" who listens to his parents and basically stays out of trouble. He watches music videos to "veg out" for a while, not really aware of all the sexual images and references being pumped into his psyche. Puberty is well underway, and he is beginning to attach sexual feelings to the visual images of seductive women. He is confused as to how he is to respond. Should he act on his feelings or suppress them? Who should he talk to: friends, parents, or sex ed teachers?

As hormone levels rise, he's excited but afraid. He has felt intense emotions before, but none quite like this. They feel potent, and he is not quite certain just how potent they are. One thing he does know is that they are affirmed wherever he goes. Sex ed classes, the locker room, guys in the shower, and larger-than-life billboards hit him with both barrels.

At home, Eric sees his parents applaud his grades and attend virtually all of his basketball games. They seem more comfortable with his athletic and intellectual abilities than with his feelings and his sexuality. They encourage his athletics and grades, and this makes him feel good. But for many reasons, they overlook engaging his feelings about his sexuality, leaving him confused about the significance and the power of those feelings.

With his male friends, Eric is eager to have approval. He is painfully vulnerable to any actions that bolster his value in the eyes of his peers. He doesn't have to listen long in the locker room or stare into the TV too long to realize a quick way to accomplish that. So he finds a girl who has no compunction about sex. Depending upon his peer subculture, he has perhaps achieved his goal. To the guys, he is cooler. He has crossed the line and lost his virginity.

Remember: Eric is painfully egocentric, living with an invisible audience waiting to critique or applaud his every thought and gesture. Sexual references, often married to athletic prowess, stream toward him constantly. Since he perceives his sexuality receiving so much attention, he concludes that sex must be HUGE.

Eric's sensibilities cry out that his intellect, emotions, and athletic abilities should be more important to others than his sexuality. Something has gone awry, and Eric wants it changed.

3. Your sexual feelings are unique in their character; they abide by different rules.

The third potent message osmotically placed in teens' minds is that their sexual feelings are unique in power and they abide by different rules than their other emotions. Of course, we adults would never teach this to our teens, but it is a very real, albeit subconscious, message that teens receive.

During the early elementary school years, our children learn appropriate behavioral interactions. Kindergartners are taught not to hit or tattletale. Conscientious teachers intervene between sparring second-grade girls, helping them talk to one another courteously rather than call names. Fourth-grade boys are directed not to put down a classmate because of a handicap or physically unpleasant appearance.

In short, we teach kids from early ages that while they experience strong emotions, they don't need to act on them. We teach our children, "Yes, I know you feel angry, but talk rather than hit."

The junior and high school years reinforce these lessons on a larger scale. Anger is fiercer, grief lasts longer, and frustration sometimes makes teens ready to explode. Teens don't know how to deal with a barrage of feelings, but we continually reinforce that while their feelings are strong, it is important to refrain from acting upon those feelings.

We would never tell our teens, "I know you're angry with your father, so go ahead and shoot him." In short, we expect our teens to restrain themselves in the midst of intense feelings simply because the consequences of acting upon them might hurt them and those around them.

Now consider our cultural approach to teen sexuality. We educated adults realize that their hormones are fluctuating and their emotions have a new power with regard to sexual involvement. Rather than embracing and directing our teens, we throw up our hands. I've seen many in my medical profession give up as well, saying, "Well, there's nothing we can do, so we better just try to keep them from having babies."

Parents taking cues from the medical profession and schools trying to keep kids "safe" during sexual activity often stay silent. The message from this adult community is, "Your sexual urges and interests abide by different rules than do your other feelings. Therefore, your sexual urges must be more powerful than other emotions."

Sexual experimentation was endorsed in the sixties and seventies, and many parents may feel glad that it was. After all, we reason, we turned out all right, didn't we?

Some parents are uncertain what to tell their kids about sexual activity—uncertain about the true physical and psychological risks. I would exhort you to simply do two things with an open mind. First, choose a well-respected internist or pediatrician in your community and make an appointment with him or her. Then pose the following question from an honest heart: "Doctor, is it healthy and good for Sarah, my sixteen-year-old daughter, to be sexually active?" Then wait for an answer.

Second, if you are still unconvinced, don't put this book down without reading chapters 12 and 13, and let me give you a peek into what we physicians are taught regarding your teenager's health. While it is my deep conviction that sexual urges should not be treated as having different rules than other feelings, I realize that some parents grapple with the impracticality of treating sexual urges in the same manner as emotional urges. We conclude, "Sure, that's reasonable. It makes sense but it just isn't practical. Kids will be kids."

To these adults, let me cast another light onto our thinking. When we examine the most troubled teens in our country, we usually look first at those in the inner cities. There we find clusters of boys armed with enough ammunition to wipe out a city block, carousing and scheming to maintain status in their gang. No one would intelligently argue that these kids are happy. They are lost, immature, and angry kids. Their anger is peppered with pain, causing them to be impulsive, confused, and violent.

I can't imagine any compassionate adult arguing that they aren't angry and in pain. Now, let us look at our response to this anger. Do we throw up our hands and state that their anger is out of control so there is no need to redirect and restrain it?

Certainly not. This response would not only be foolish for the larger communities but cold and inhumane to the kids. We have churches, local agencies, and Big Brother and Big Sister programs intervening with inner-city teens for the purpose of helping them deal with painful feelings and change their behavior.

Why should we respond any differently when it comes to their sexual behavior? Can we argue that their sexual urges are stronger than the emotions of abandonment and grief? Certainly not. It is not sexual urges that are creating gangs or making kids run away or even causing teen boys to rape girls. It is deep pain, deep anger, and very tangled responses to these feelings. Anger is more powerful than sexual urges.

If we expect anger to be embraced and we work to help teens refrain from acting upon it, why then do we treat sexual urges differently? We can no longer treat them as more powerful and permit them to abide by different rules.

Beginning the preservation or restoration of our teens means recognizing the messages they perceive from us and their immediate culture regarding their sexuality. It also means understanding that directing their sexuality is crucial to restoring our teens' dignity because their sexuality is intimately entwined with their physical, psychological, and even their spiritual health.

Chapter Eleven

BROKEN BODIES

Part of my pediatric residency training included work dubbed "transport call" by my peers. Transport call was reserved for senior residents assigned to leave our hospital via ambulance, retrieve seriously ill children from outlying hospitals, and return them to our pediatric hospital for specialized care. Transport call was my least favorite part of training. For one, I was terrified of speeding ambulances and secondly, being responsible for a deathly ill child without familiar nursing staff and ancillary services was unnerving at best.

Late one Saturday evening, a transport call request came through. Two hours away at another medical facility, a five-year-old boy lay in a coma after sustaining a fall at home. I wondered, *What kind of fall at midnight?* The details were unknown, but I was requested to come right away.

Armed with clipboard, supplies, and curiosity, I followed the emergency medical team into the ambulance and scooted down the highway in pelting rain. Deep unsettled feelings surfaced as I reviewed various treatment plans for anticipated medical complications. When the ambulance parked beneath a sheltered emergency room exit, I nervously jumped out and followed an attendant through a course of automatic doors. Turning briskly to the left, I will never forget the sight.

Partially clothed and quietly supine, Danny lay extended on a steel examining table. His body was quiet, disturbed but motionless. His puffy eyes were shut, and a plastic endotracheal tube protruded from his throat to help him breathe. Thick curly black hair framed his face, and his cheeks were a glossy caramel color. The skin around his scalp was perfectly intact.

I placed my stethoscope over his clean chest and heard the easy, mechanical puffs of air from the ventilator. As I listened, my eyes drifted to his abdomen, where I noticed a peculiar marking across his belly. Gently I removed my stethoscope and placed my hands over his abdomen, first feeling for deep abdominal injuries, then tracing the skin marking with my fingers. It resembled a belt buckle.

Realizing his condition was stable, I removed his clothing, pants, underwear, and socks in search of clues regarding "the fall." I discovered a bruise on the buttocks, a couple of faded ones near his ear. Rage and nausea welled in me. These feelings wouldn't leave as I stabilized Danny and designated medical maneuvers.

I entered the visitor's lounge to speak with his mother. She sat tensely beside a man along the back wall. Three chairs removed sat a little girl about two years old, resembling Danny.

I introduced myself to his mother and asked the usual questions.

"Can you tell me what happened to Danny earlier tonight?" I began.

"I'm not really sure," she replied listlessly. "I was at work. I guess he just fell in the bathtub. My boyfriend was there when he just fell and hit his head when he was getting out of the tub."

The fact that she failed to address her boyfriend by name made we question how well she knew this fellow. I looked directly at his face. He glared back.

"Sir, how did Danny fall in the tub?" I seethed.

"Don't know—I didn't see him. Told him to take a bath and go to bed. That's what he did. Just fell against the side, I guess, when he was gettin' out. I just found him lying there, and we brought him in."

My attention turned briefly to the little girl in the corner, then back to the mother and boyfriend. Ten more minutes of questioning, ten minutes of vague and frustrating replies.

I returned to Danny's side, and the emergency room nurse announced the arrival of processed CAT scan films. Appropriately, the ER staff had taken a CAT scan of Danny's head before I arrived. More clues hung on the wall overlying the white lit box. I looked at pictures of Danny's brain.

Peculiarly, his skull was fine, but the films revealed massive swelling of vital parts of his brain. *We've got to hurry and get him back* was all I thought. I directed the staff to pack him up and prepare for departure.

The portable ventilator puffed air rhythmically and peacefully into Danny's lungs as we bounded down the highway, sirens on full blast.

I looked at the belt mark and recalled the earlier excuse regarding its origin. Then the buttock and facial marks. Again, the same empty lies. Clearly, Danny's little body had been brutalized, and his coma was due not to a bathtub but by larger and more powerful limbs. The sad truth was that even if he were able to speak, Danny probably wouldn't divulge the truth. He would have been too terrified.

Suddenly, the alarm on the heart rate and blood pressure monitor sounded. My heart fell. *No! Not here! Not on the highway!* I realized that his brain was shifting beneath his skull. Within this flying, dark, and eerie ambulance, Danny might die.

Please God, I thought, *don't let Danny die.* Danny stabilized, and my worry quickened to anger. I was furious with his mother and hated her boyfriend. I felt sorry for Danny's sister.

Over the ensuing days in our intensive care unit, the police and Child Protective Services social workers interrogated the mother and her boyfriend. Danny fought for his life, but he never recovered from his injuries. He died in his sleep.

There have been few times in my medical career when I wanted to quit, but Danny's death was one of them. Danny didn't deserve to die, especially after I learned the details of what really happened.

Danny's mom was single, probably abused herself. She lived with Danny and his sister as boyfriends came and went. This particular live-in, fresh from his own teen years, was heavily involved with drugs—predominantly crack cocaine. His usage had increased with the stress of watching after the kids while the mother worked. He had no job, and he used crack to cover the pain.

Did he kill Danny? I'm afraid we'll never know. His death was recorded as "unspecified trauma of unknown origin." Yet we can safely assume that drugs killed Danny. The boyfriend's drug use contributed to a mood-altered rage that escalated out of control, and it's certain that his drug use began in his teenage days.

More Than Statistics

Let's look for a moment at drugs and our teenagers. First of all, I dislike citing statistics because of a common human response to them. When we read statistics, our eyes glaze over and we tend to remove ourselves and our teens from the numbers. Why? Because we don't want to see either ourselves or our children as a statistic. We don't want to consider that perhaps our teens are involved in destructive behavior. But we mustn't allow our reluctance to hinder us from helping our kids. Our teens can't afford our inability to accept truth.

Research tells us that too many of our teens choose to alter reality via drugs or alcohol. Our country enjoyed a decrease in drug abuse during the 1980s, but that changed during the 1990s. The National Institute of Drug Abuse performed a survey in 1993 and 1994 revealing that 40 percent of seniors in high school used marijuana within the preceding year.

Other reports cite marijuana as the most commonly used illicit drug among seventh through twelfth graders, with 28 percent of kids using it. About one third use any illicit drugs, 11 percent use stimulants, 6 percent cocaine, and 6 percent inhalants.[17]

Alcohol is the most common drug of choice for teens, however, and teens aren't drinking just one or two drinks at a time. Research points toward binge drinking patterns among teens. The 1993 Monitoring the Future Survey showed that 28 percent of high school seniors admitted to having five or more drinks in a row on at least one occasion in the two weeks prior to the survey![18] Medical data illuminates a frightening trend toward alcohol abuse in teens. One large study showed that 90 percent of high school students have tried alcohol, more than 50 percent are current users, and 28 percent binge drink.[19]

Now combine this with a few other sobering facts about drug and alcohol abuse. Teens, unlike adults, tend to use alcohol (beer and wine) as a "gateway" drug; that is, once they start drinking, they often progress to using hard liquor, marijuana, and other drugs.

Cigarettes and inhalants are also gateway drugs. Inhalants can be anything from glue, correction fluid, gasoline, butane, freon, and ether, to name a few. Inhalant use has been found to peak among eighth-grade students. This is probably due to the easy availability of inhalants (many can be found around the home), as well as naiveté of the early adolescent mindset regarding the harmful consequences of inhalant use.

Teens often start with the gateway drugs and progress to harder ones such as:

❖ stimulants (speed, crank, ice)

❖ hard liquor

❖ hallucinogens such as LSD (acid)

❖ PCP (angel dust)

❖ cocaine

❖ heroin and prescription opiates (codeine, Percocet)[20]

Teens, unlike adults, tend to continue using previous drugs as they progress upward in strength. Thus, they take numerous substances at one time. In addition, early use of drugs during the pre-adolescent and adolescent years correlates to later drug use. The boyfriend caring for Danny probably began using drugs early on and continued through his teen years and into early adulthood.

What are the risk factors for teens using drugs? There are many, but the following are the most common:

❖ a parent or relative with a substance abuse problem

❖ low achievement (especially in school)

❖ poor self-esteem

❖ aggressive personality (ADHD kids are at higher risk)

❖ family instability (divorce or severe dysfunction)

❖ history of sexual or physical abuse

❖ psychological disorders, especially depression[21]

What are the protective factors? Here's the good news: there are some very important ones, and we will look at them in greater detail in the next few chapters. The main protective factors identified through research are the following:

❖ family connectedness

❖ school connectedness

❖ perceived importance of religion and prayer

❖ high levels of self-esteem[22]

BLAIR'S STORY

My first introduction to Blair occurred early one particular Monday morning at my office. His mother and I were friends, and she filled me in on the details of his life as most female friends do. School was up and down: academic and athletic achievements intermixed with failing classes.

I had mixed emotions about seeing Blair. At first, I wanted to suggest that he see another physician, wondering if I could be objective enough, but I had learned medical objectivity living in a small town, so I took Blair under my care.

"Good morning," I began during our very first one-on-one conversation.

"Hi," offered Blair.

"I'm glad to get a chance to know you better. I feel like I already know you in some ways, but I only get to hear about your life through your mom's eyes. I'm glad to hear about it from your perspective."

"Yeah, I guess so." Blair, quite understandably, was not wanting to connect. Perhaps it was because he knew I was another one of his mom's friends, but the sadness and anxiety on Blair's face prompted me to just dive in.

"Blair, this is an incredibly tough time for you. I know. I can see it on your face. Before we start, I want you to know that whatever you say stays in this room. I know I am your mom's friend, but you are my number-one priority now, not my friendship with your mother, so let's put that aside. I need you to be honest with me so I can help you feel better. If you're too uncomfortable, let me know. If you want me to help or if you'd feel better with someone else, I'll help you find another doctor."

Blair unfolded his arms and dropped them from his chest to his lap. "No," he said. "It doesn't matter. This is okay." At least we had begun to take a step forward. I was glad.

I continued to press into uncomfortable areas.

"Tell me what was going on during the last week you spent at school," I inquired.

Blair had left home and was attending a new high school out of state. He was an excellent athlete and had left home to play at a school that afforded him the opportunity to excel athletically. I knew his parents had agonized over this decision, and it was a big move for the family.

"I don't know. I just was feeling really down. Exams were coming up, and I was having trouble studying. This girl I'd been seeing wanted to bag out of our relationship. It just seemed like everything was just kind of piling up all at once."

"Do you have any friends you could talk to?"

"Yeah. I've got a lot of nice friends. Mostly girls. Some guys. Everybody's got a lot of problems. School's really tough."

"What do you do when things get tough, Blair? Do you feel comfortable about talking to anybody about things being rough?"

"Kind of," he started. "I talk to a few kids, but I don't know, not about some stuff."

"What kind of stuff is some stuff?"

"I don't know. I just felt all squeezed in. My coach was on me, my girlfriend was freaking out, and I just started drinking more."

"How did drinking make you feel?"

"Better—for a while. But it's a real downer when it's over. I couldn't get my work done, and I was gettin' farther behind. Hey—you're not gonna tell Mom are you?"

"Blair, what you say to me is confidential. I will tell her only what you say is all right to tell her. Remember?"

"Yeah, but she doesn't know I drink. It would kill her."

"Blair, I think your Mom knows you're hurting. She knows about the slit on your wrist. She's handling that, isn't she?"

"That's another thing. I just feel so guilty. I'm wrecking my parents' lives. They're trying hard, and I'm blowing it. In some ways I wish I'd succeeded."

Blair sat still for several seconds before he continued. "Well, no, I guess I'm glad it didn't work. I don't think I really wanted to die. It's embarrassing, you know."

"When did you start drinking?" I continued.

"Well, let's see, eighth grade, no, maybe ninth." He felt more comfortable now, almost relaxed. Blair seemed somewhat relieved to get everything out into the open.

"Ninth grade? How'd you get started?"

"Oh, I don't know. Me and my friends would just fool around at somebody's house. A few of us guys did it just for fun. You know, after practice we'd hang out, watch TV, and have a few beers. It was a kick."

"Is it still a kick, Blair?"

"Yeah, I like it. Most of the time. Sometimes it makes me do stupid stuff. But you know, drinking calms me down. When I get all tight and jumpy on the inside, drinking calms me down."

Over the next ninety minutes, Blair described the ebb and flow of his previous two years. He began drinking "just for fun," eventually spending his free time exclusively with a few drinking friends. Blair had become a teenage alcoholic who frequently lied to friends and family. He was clever at hiding. Moving out of state made hiding easier. Alcohol became his normal coping mechanism for stress—from athletics, from academics, from uncomfortable feelings, and from the breakup of a girlfriend. The buzz of a few drinks was enough to entice him to cash it all in.

In the early morning hours several days before our visit, Blair slit one wrist. The depth of the scar made it clear that this was more than a gesture. He had a deeper desire to kill himself. A close friend intercepted him and called for help.

Blair's family history appeared normal. His parents were married. His father made a healthy income, which afforded his mother to stay at home full time. He had siblings, went to church, and was active in his athletic pursuits. Perhaps he had succeeded too much. A deeper look at his life reveals a lack of failing at anything. His grades were always excellent, as were his athletic accomplishments. His mother and father, in their zeal for his achievements, communicated too much emphasis on what he did rather than who he was. Blair felt great internal pressure to succeed for them, and he hated it. He was terrified of failing—even a pop quiz.

As I dug further, I learned that Blair had an alcoholic grandfather and had seen his own father drink on occasion. Thus, he was at a higher risk for developing a substance abuse problem. He had struggled on and off during his early adolescent years with depression, setting him up for trying mind-altering substances. He was introduced to drinking by a few friends in the eighth grade, and he had cleverly hid this from his parents, as most kids do.

When he went away to school, he was ripe for substance abuse since he had established a "friendship" with alcohol (and a few other drugs he used on occasion). When he broke from his family and encountered school-related stress, his depression escalated and the lure of alcohol's deadening effect proved too great. Alcohol initially helped his mood, but as the effect wore off, he found himself more depressed. Thus, the abusive cycle began and the combination of depression, alcohol, and distance from family combined to nearly kill Blair.

Our teens are up against a brutal and contradicting culture. As professionals assess and research "health risk factors," we see the marriage of alcohol, drug and tobacco use, violence, emotional distress, and sexual activity. Teens like Blair receive continually mixed messages regarding the dangers and the pleasures of those things, so they test a few and see where they lead.

Unfortunately, most lead to deeper emotional or physical distress. In fact, the main threat to an adolescent's health in the second decade of life are suicides, homicides, and accidents. Eighty percent of teen deaths are due to one of these, and in half of these cases, drugs or alcohol are involved.

But we adults can make changes for our teens and for these statistics. A comprehensive national study on adolescent health stated, "Of the constellation of forces that influence adolescent health-risk behavior, the most fundamental are the social contexts in which adolescents are embedded; the family and school contexts are among the most critical."[23]

We'll study this statement further in the next chapter.

Chapter Twelve

SHE WASN'T WELL AT ALL

Already our bodies are fallen, bruised, badly bruised
Already our souls are oozing through the exit
Of the cruel bruise.

D.H. LAWRENCE

RACHEL WAS PHYSICALLY STUNNING. WHEN I FIRST LOOKED AT her eyes in the examination room, I glanced a few moments longer in an attempt to distinguish the blackness of her pupils from the surrounding chocolate iris.

Her face, I noticed, didn't have the usual peppering of teenage acne. She saw fit to refrain from piercing more than once in each earlobe, and her nose was unscarred. She wore her elbow-length, Asian-black hair parted on the side. When she cocked her head, her hair covered a portion of her face.

As her physician and friend, I was glad she lived in Michigan. Surely, I surmised, some Hollywood type would have spotted her and positioned her beauty for his own profit if she lived on the West Coast.

"Rachel, how are you?" I began.

She barely raised her brows from their cocked position. I could see she was not well. Not well at all.

"Rachel, tell me something . . . what's wrong?" I tried to sound comforting rather than demanding.

Rachel cried quietly, then intensely, then quietly again.

"I promise—I'm here to help you," I soothed. "Please let me help." I knew she was frightened and afraid to talk.

Shortly, her crying stopped. She regained her composure, lifted her head, and adopted a defensive posture. Her tears dried up.

"I did it again, but something's gone wrong."

"What's gone wrong, Rachel?" I was pretty sure what she was talking about, but I needed certainty and details.

"You know, this is my third one, but I'm bleeding real bad—he botched it." Her face was now colder, her chocolate eyes empty. I felt as though I'd been kicked in the stomach.

"When was it done?" I quietly asked. I had seen abortions go wrong before.

"Two days ago, and I just won't stop bleeding," she answered. "I don't understand what's going on. Do you think he finished it?"

"No, Rachel, I don't think he finished your abortion." I hurt for Rachel. She was seventeen, bleeding profusely through her vagina, and my anger fused with frustration and hurt, realizing that this was one medical complication I was poorly equipped to handle. Rachel needed surgical intervention, and I wasn't a surgeon.

For several moments, she wouldn't tell me which doctor performed her evacuation. I needed to know because good medical practice dictates that if complications arise from a surgical procedure, the original physician who performed the procedure follows up to care for complications. I needed his name so I could call him to take care of the problem.

Rachel finally gave his name, and when I called and identified myself, I was informed that he was unable to see her. Finally, we got Rachel into the hands of a skilled ob-gyn to stem the bleeding.

What happened? During Rachel's third abortion, she experienced a dangerous situation. While no one was exactly sure how far along she was, she had retained a portion of her placenta after the procedure was finished. When the placenta stays in the uterus, vaginal bleeding continues and uterine infection can occur. Rachel was in the early stages. The infection, if not treated, could progress into the blood-stream and circulate throughout the body, with death ensuing.

Rachel didn't succumb that day. After committing her to the care of a good ob-gyn physician, she didn't suffer complications other than blood loss. Caring for post-abortion patients can be a medical night-mare. Rachel's original surgeon didn't want to follow up on her medical complications; I'm not sure why. Other gynecologists refused to see Rachel because of their ethical beliefs. I was not medically quali-fied to scrape out her uterine lining. Rachel's mother didn't even know she had the abortion (or the previous two), and Rachel didn't want to recruit her help. Not only was the situation a medical disaster, it was emotionally traumatic for Rachel as well. No wonder her eyes had grown cold.

Where had Rachel gone wrong? Perhaps I could have helped her in our early visits by setting standards for her. When she intellectual-ized her reasons for being sexually active, I nodded and encouraged her to use oral contraceptives—the newest with the least side-effects of breast tenderness, weight gain, and mid-cycle bleeding.

After dispensing oral contraceptives, I strongly urged her to have her partners use condoms, but she told me she didn't like any type of "unnatural" intervention. My failure was not in choice of medication; it was a lack of engagement. What Rachel needed was a heart-to-heart confrontation regarding her sexual decisions.

The truth was, she confided later, she didn't really like sex. Furthermore, she didn't have a steady boyfriend and alluded to a variety of superficial reasons for being sexually involved. Rachel cried out for permission to refrain from sexual activity, but she never heard it from me.

Emotionally charged debates rise up surrounding the issue of abortion. I am convinced that if those condoning abortions could witness one or two of them, their minds would be swayed. But with arguments aside, let us return to Rachel. Clearly, her body and soul had not been served well. Her health had been failed by an immediate culture withholding truthful information regarding the consequences of her decisions.

ELLEN'S TENDER SPIRIT

When Ellen left my practice and returned home to go off to college, I was excited but afraid for her. She was bright, assertive—but ashamed. Ellen was the type of young woman who didn't stand out in a crowd. Her gentle face was pretty but not beautiful. She was trim from disciplined eating and a strict exercise regimen. Her white-blond hair had deepened to a mud color, and the mixture of blue and green in her eyes looked more brown than blue.

Ellen had a tender spirit beneath her controlled demeanor. Over the years, I came to know her well, but her guardedness always kept me and others at a safe distance. One day, I believed she would let someone close.

Ellen first came to see me during her pre-adolescent years for a handful of checkups. During the summer between her eighth- and ninth-grade years, Ellen arrived for an appointment. As I customarily do with girls who are Ellen's age, I offered her the option of a physical exam with or without her mother present. She opted for the latter, and her mother excused herself politely.

During my exam I began questioning her menstrual cycles, what her friends were like, or anything else she might feel uncomfortable discussing in her mother's presence. At first she was quiet. When I finished my exam and began writing notes in her chart, she blurted, "I've got a boyfriend."

"Oh, what's his name?" I inquired.

"Brad." Again she became silent but anxious. I knew she wanted to continue so I waited.

"How old is Brad?" I asked.

"Seventeen."

"Oh—that must make him a junior this fall, right?"

"Yup."

Ellen withdrew and tucked her hands beneath her thighs, pressing down on her palms. I sensed that she wanted to talk, so I opened up. "Ellen, are you and Brad having sex together?"

"Sometimes." I thought the words would continue more easily, but they didn't.

"Ellen, do you want to be sexually active with Brad?" I asked.

"Oh, I dunno. It's all right, I guess. He's nice, but you know—sex isn't what it's cracked up to be."

Ellen and I talked about her feelings, her likes and dislikes, and her behavior as deeply as one can with a fourteen-year-old mind. She admitted she was confused, but wasn't sure she would be able to refrain from sex with Brad. She finally admitted she didn't even like sex, but didn't see a way to stop doing it. When I asked her if she wanted some condoms, she replied that they were "gross" and Brad didn't like them either. Besides, she didn't want any because she wanted to stop having sex with Brad. I was glad she felt that way.

Eventually, Ellen broke up with Brad but continued to be in and out of relationships with different boys, usually older than she. I saw Ellen infrequently, and during her last visit before she left for college, I told her I needed to perform a gynecological exam. She complied readily.

When the test results returned from the specimens I took, I informed Ellen that she had a chlamydial infection along with an abnormal pap smear. I treated her infection and sent her for further testing by our ob-gyn. He diagnosed Ellen with early cancer of the cervix.

Ellen underwent surgical procedures to burn portions of her cervix affected by the early cancer. She was informed that the cause of cervical cancer in the vast majority of cases is HPV-human papilloma virus. She learned that she would require much more frequent gynecological exams and continued close scrutiny of her cervix.

In college, Ellen contracted genital herpes type II, and she experienced deep shame, as most people do.[24] She continued to be sexually promiscuous, however, subjecting herself—in spite of oral contraceptives (which she eventually did use) and occasional condoms—to a multitude of sexually transmitted diseases and their complications.

Unfortunately for Ellen, these were the least of her problems. She plummeted into depression, which required medical intervention and intense psychotherapy. Through the unraveling of her emotions and thought processes, her behavior made perfect sense.

At age eleven, Ellen had been sexually assaulted by an older family member. No one knew except Ellen and the man. Her subsequent sexual behavior reflected a young woman in anguish—physically and emotionally. These scars should not be part of the normal teenager experience.

The best medical literature available concerning sexually transmitted diseases and their complications has been compiled and reviewed by the Medical Institute in Austin, Texas. As mentioned before, the Institute was founded in the mid-1990s for the purpose of educating the public about the rising epidemic of sexually transmitted diseases striking young adults around the world. Much of the following data was compiled by the Medical Institute.

As loosely as we educators talk about chlamydia, others receive inference that perhaps it has been around for decades. In fact, chlamydia was first discovered to cause genital infections as recently as

1976.[25] It was a rare problem back then, and in nearly twenty-five years, chlamydia has become the most common STD in the United States.

Chlamydia can cause an infection of the cervix, uterus, fallopian tubes, or ovaries. Teens like Ellen are much more susceptible to sexually transmitted diseases like chlamydia because the lining of the teen cervix produces more mucus, which in turn provides nourishment for the bacteria or virus. In addition, up to half of all girls who menstruate fail to ovulate during the first two years of their cycle. This lack of ovulation during the menstrual cycles causes the cervical mucus to be thinner and more liquid, allowing a better environment in which bacteria and viruses can thrive.

One of the most serious aspects of chlamydial infections is the fact that they are often asymptomatic. Since chlamydia easily ascends the female reproductive tract, it can infect the fallopian tubes and ovaries and still remain asymptomatic. Often women discover that a chlamydial infection has occurred only after they try to get pregnant and fail. That's when the attending physician finds that their fallopian tubes have been permanently scarred.

Fortunately Ellen's chlamydial infection was localized to her cervix, but in many other women it goes on to cause full-blown pelvic inflammatory disease, or PID. When it does cause PID, the risk of infertility is high. About 75 percent of women who have had chlamydial PID will require treatment (often surgery) if they desire to become pregnant.[26] One single infection produces about a 25 percent chance of infertility, and the second infection produces about 50 percent infertility.[27]

The treatment for chlamydial infections is antibiotics, a treatment that is not always successful. In addition, studies have shown that teens fail to respond as well to antibiotic treatment as adults and may require major surgery down the road.[28]

Now consider the fact that further studies reveal that some 20 percent to 40 percent of sexually active singles are infected[29] and we begin to realize how sobering this silent disease can be. It struck Ellen—from all appearances a lovely, well-adjusted teen—in the prime of her life.

Another silent disease is the human papilloma virus (HPV). HPV is responsible for more than 90 percent of all precancerous lesions of the cervix.[30] As recently as 1995, cervical cancer was taking more lives of women than AIDS.[31] HPV infections like other sexually transmitted diseases can be more aggressive in teens than older women. Since cervical cancer is the second most common cancer among women worldwide and it is directly related to sexual activity, we realize how important it is to help our teen girls stay away from danger.

While HPV causes silent damage to internal organs, it is also responsible for genital warts on young men as well as young women. These venereal warts can become quite large and must be treated with either medication or surgery.

Ellen didn't know she had HPV. She didn't know about cervical cancer. Her first introduction came after that abnormal precancerous pap smear at age eighteen. After further evaluation, her gynecologist performed a "conization." This procedure involves burning a cone-shaped slice into the cervix with a laser instrument, which allows a sizable portion of her cervix—the precancerous area—to slough off.

Historically, precancerous lesions showed up in middle-aged and older women. But since the Sexual Revolution and the advent of increased circulation of numerous strains of the human papilloma virus, precancerous cervical lesions are raging like a brush fire through the teen population. Sadly, they appear not in the practices of internists and family practitioners, but in those like mine—pediatric offices.

Let's look at herpes and AIDS. When I was in medical school in the early 1980s, herpes was dubbed the "yuppie" disease. In October 1997, the *New England Journal of Medicine* published a study showing how common herpes is becoming in the U.S. The article explained that since the late 1970's herpes type II has increased 30 percent and is now detected in one out of every five people twelve years of age and older nationwide.[32]

Once a patient contracts herpes, he has it for life, not knowing when the genital lesions will erupt. Fortunately, medicine is available to control most outbreaks, but once the antiviral medication is stopped, the outbreaks recur.

HERPES: A HORRIBLE DISEASE

Herpes is extraordinarily humiliating. I remember being called to the delivery of a colleague's baby. She had active genital herpes at the time of delivery, so her baby was born by a Cesarean section since a herpes infection could be devastating to her baby. Her obstetrician removed her beautiful little boy from her belly, passed him to me, and we placed the baby in isolation in the nursery. While her baby did well physically, his incubator was stamped with signs warning caretakers of his condition. This was necessary hospital procedure to protect other infants from potentially contracting a herpes infection-passed perhaps by one brief sexual encounter between two young adults many years before.

A painful disease, herpes can kill babies and makes its victims feel terrible about themselves. When questioned, the vast majority of carriers report that they felt less confident about themselves. They feel "contaminated," "less desirable sexually," and "depressed."[33]

While herpes is a horrible disease, it still pales to the dreaded HIV virus, the precursor to AIDS. Let's review where we stand amidst the AIDS epidemic. In March 1995, the *Journal of the American Medical Association (JAMA)* reported an update on AIDS among women from the Centers for Disease Control and Prevention. They wrote that "HIV/AIDS was the fourth-leading cause of death among women aged 25-44 years in the United States."

Young women are experiencing an increased incidence of infection with HIV. A report from Drs. Wortley and Fleming states, "Between 1991 and 1995, the number of women diagnosed as having acquired immunodeficiency syndrome (AIDS) increased by 63 percent. Much of this rise has been due to heterosexual contact."[34]

For African Americans, AIDS is on the rise. The CDC reported, "In 1995, for the first time, the proportion of persons reported with AIDS who are black was equal to the proportion who are white." HIV is the leading cause of death among black males fifteen to forty-four years of age.[35]

In March 1997, *JAMA* published news that the CDC was reporting 68,473 AIDS cases during 1996, a substantially higher number (47 percent) than the number reported from 1992. *Forty-seven percent higher in four years.* Note the following from the same report: "The largest proportionate increase in AIDS from June 1995 through June 1996 occurred among persons infected through heterosexual contact (19 percent)." Remember that while not all people infected with HIV develop AIDS, most do. And once AIDS appears, victims always die.

Viruses, like the HIV, reproduce as they circulate. During this reproduction, viruses can change their character or "mutate." Bacterial mutation has occurred, providing bacterial strains (i.e., Group A streptococcus) that "outsmart" antibiotics and become resistant to them. Thus, medical research continues to target these mutated strains in order to produce antibiotics that could kill or slow the activity of these new strains.

HIV has the same potential for mutation as other viruses and bacteria, and this makes its presence and activity even more alarming to medical researchers. When we consider that between one and two million Americans are infected, the possibility for HIV transmission is sobering at best.

Finally, let us shed light on two other sexually transmitted diseases that generally go unnoticed: hepatitis B and gonorrhea. Immunization programs have recently bolstered efforts to immunize against hepatitis B from birth. Immunization efforts erupted from the knowledge that hepatitis B is a preventable disease and that children were at risk, particularly during the teen years.

Most people don't realize that hepatitis B is considered a sexually transmitted disease and kills between 5,000 and 6,000 Americans each year.[36] Hepatitis B is about eight times as efficient as HIV in transmission. The United States actually fares better than other countries regarding prevalence; the CDC reported in 1992 that 300 million people worldwide were infected.[37] Hepatitis B remains a prominent STD with complications of chronic hepatitis, cirrhosis and liver cancer. There are approximately 200,000 *new* Hepatitis B infections in the U.S. per year, and half are transmitted through intercourse.[38]

Gonorrhea and syphilis, while not receiving the publicity of chlamydia and HIV, still thrive. Both gonorrhea and syphilis are responsible for causing PID and scarring, even with medical treatment. The CDC reported in 1995 that "Infections due to Neisseria gonorrhea, like those due to chlamydia trachomatis, remain a major cause of PID, tubal infertility, ectopic pregnancy and chronic pelvic pain in the United States.[39] Males may suffer from urethral stricture as well as urinary and ejaculatory problems resulting from scarring caused by syphilis.

Syphilis continues to spread quickly throughout the United States, and many teens who have syphilis may not even know it. Babies can contract syphilis in utero through their mother. This is called congenital syphilis, which can cause devastating problems to babies. If a mother is not treated, 20 percent of babies will be either stillborn or miscarried and 15 percent of those born will die shortly after birth.[40] Also, 33 percent will have permanent brain or body damage.[41] From 1984-1993, congenital syphilis (babies born with syphilis) increased twelvefold.[42]

Fortunately, the United States has seen a decrease in the overall number of cases of syphilis, but physicians, educators and parents must not become complacent because syphilis still remains one of the most commonly reported infectious diseases in the U.S.[43] Syphilis can be transmitted through kissing as well as through sexual intercourse and unfortunately, about one half of patients infected with syphilis are unaware of its presence.[44]

Sexually transmitted diseases threaten the health of our teens in numbers that our culture has never seen before. *We have an epidemic on our hands. We now have more than 25 significant STDs. Before 1960, we had two—syphilis and gonorrhea.* As we enter the milennium, 87 percent of all reportable communicable diseases in the U.S. are caused by STDs.[45] The faces of STDs includes Ellen and many of my patients—and may include your son or daughter. If infected, they won't know it until they have an abnormal pap smear or urethral discharge. Perhaps our adult thinking prevents us from believing our children will be one of the statistics. We feel we got through those promiscuous years unscathed, so what's the big deal?

The big deal is 12 million Americans—*3 million of whom are teens*—who get a new STD every year.[46] One of these teens may be your son or daughter, and many will be my patients. In addition to a broken body, each will endure emotional pain, confusion, and perhaps even death. Adults armed with medical facts about the cost of alcohol abuse, sexually transmitted diseases, and drug usage *can and must* intercede for our young people. Arming teens with knowledge regarding risk factors is important, but even more critical is teaching them how to change behavior patterns that may get them into trouble.

Remember, we must intercede one teen at a time to influence their behavior.

Chapter Thirteen

BROKEN HEARTS

WHEN I COMPLETED MY PEDIATRIC RESIDENCY TRAINING IN 1987 and headed toward the world of private practice, I was well-versed in medically managing a variety of illnesses from diabetic comas to seizure disorders. I was fortunate to train at Children's Hospital in Milwaukee, granting me exposure to a vast assortment of maladies.

Private practitioners like myself were trained to take care of the kidneys and lungs, while psychiatrists took care of the human mind. We prescribed insulin, they prescribed Ritalin. We manipulated antibiotics, they treated nervous breakdown. When I first began practicing, I felt quite comfortable amidst alarms in the intensive care unit, but I was frightened of kids who couldn't think clearly.

Between 1984 and 1994, the world of medicine changed dramatically for me and other practitioners with the advancement of medical understanding and treatment of psychiatric disorders. This has been fortunate since the volume of patients suffering from these disorders has increased dramatically. Attention deficit hyperactivity disorder (ADHD), for instance, is one ailment no longer treated just by psychiatrists. We primary care physicians treat ADHD as commonly as asthma.

In addition, adolescent depression has arisen out of the wood-work. At first I thought our practice had a propensity to attract those seeking help from emotional and psychological hurts, but soon I realized that our practice wasn't really unique. Fortunately for all practitioners, the pharmaceutical market was introducing sophisticated anti-depressants—one after another. By the 1990s, Ritalin, Wellbutrin, Serzone, and Dexedrine became familiar weapons in our pediatric arsenal.

Medical literature affirms my personal experience. As we have increased our understanding of emotional disturbances, we began treating more teens. Has treatment of depression simply improved, or has the prevalence of depression risen among teens? Sadly, I believe that depression has increased amongst our teen population in the United States.

The prevalence of depression is estimated to be 25 to 60 percent of the general population of teenagers.[47] Depression is less common before puberty and rises sharply during the teen years, when thoughts of suicide arise. In a *Morbidity and Mortality Weekly Report* from 1996, nearly one in every four students reported that they had seriously considered suicide.[48] As has been shown in other research, female students are more likely to consider suicide, yet male students are more likely to succeed than girls.[49]

DEPRESSION

Depression in teens manifests itself differently than in adults. While adults may become sullen and lose interest in pleasurable activities, teens display depression upside down. They may have temper tantrums, begin disobeying parents when previously compliant, start letting their grades drop, and begin lashing out at parents, peers, or teachers. Unfortunately for many parents and physicians, detective work is often needed to uncover depression.

Psychologically, depression in teens is about loss. When a loss occurs, whether real or perceived, humans are wired with a natural and healthy grieving process. The loss is at first denied. Anger is then felt, followed by grief, and finally acceptance and resolution. We have all experienced this healthy process at one time or another. When losses are small, they are easier to accept and resolve. But as the loss increases in significance, the grief process is more painful to endure.

When this grief process is interrupted, teens adapt several coping mechanisms, but few of them are healthy. For instance, suppose sixteen-year-old Sally breaks up with her boyfriend of nine months. She will grieve the loss of his friendship and may experience diminished self-worth (girls often feel guilty and responsible for a breakup).

Depending upon her personality, Sally may grieve for a short time or a long time, but she will feel a loss because she is wired to. If her parents see her sadness but dismiss her loss, the natural progression of her grief may be interrupted. If her parents try to deny her feelings with comments like, "Honey, you only dated him nine months, so don't worry about it. There'll be other boys", then her parents cause her grief to remain in the denial stage. Again, depending upon her personality, she will either stuff her feelings or move forth and grieve them to completion. If she proceeds, resolution of the grief may take several days to several weeks, according to the depth of loss she felt.

Let's imagine Sally agrees with her parents' comments, and those comments are affirmed by her peers. Why might she do this? Many reasons. Commonly, teens will sacrifice their own feelings in order to please their parents. Remember, bridging from adolescence to adulthood requires separate behavior and separate feelings from parents. Separate behavior is easier to assume than separate feelings, and certainly behaving differently is much safer than feeling differently from parents.

My purpose is not to malign Sally's parents; in fact, they probably thought they were helping her. But their perspective of her relationship with her boyfriend was markedly different from her perspective.

Sally, submerging her feelings, continued with her usual school activities, playing soccer, and attending band practice, but within three months she began bringing new friends around the house. First she brought Annie, a classmate with five earrings in her left earlobe and two in her right nostril. Annie peppered her speech with four-letter words. Mom and Dad didn't say anything at first, but when Sally began breaking curfew and sneaking out at night, they became alarmed and sought help.

Was Sally depressed? Yes. Red flags for depression in teens, remember, aren't simply prolonged melancholia or changes in appetite and sleep. Depression can be signaled by sudden changes in behavior or changes in peer groups. Remember, depression is about loss and is often about an interrupted grief process.

What happened with Sally? The breakup of her boyfriend triggered a barrage of deep sadness. The breakup might not have caused depression, but it certainly triggered it. In fact, the pattern with which Sally handled her feelings caused her depression. Each time she felt angry or sad, Sally pushed her feelings inward, causing them to fester. When the breakup came, she tried to ignore her feelings, forcing her hurt inward. Since there was no room inside, too many other feelings of anger and hurt occupied space in her heart.

Sally's mishandling of her loss was a common pattern perpetuated within her family structure. Subconsciously Sally wouldn't let her parents see her anger and hurt for fear she "might disappoint them or look stupid." When her anger did manifest itself, she chose to change friends, and in a self-fulfilled prophetic manner she surrounded herself with behavior and friends that proved to her how stupid she really was.

Oddly, hurting teens often feel ashamed. These shameful feelings fuel aberrant behavior, which deepens their sense of shame. Anger causes them to search for a landing place for that anger. Sometimes the anger lands upon parents, siblings, or peers, but usually it lands back upon themselves.

Interrupted grief causes anger and hurt to stick within the teenage heart. Recurrent episodes of interrupted grief pile within the heart and cause tearing. The heart does not strengthen but weakens into numbness. While the heart becomes numb, the anger ascends, spilling forth rage from the teen.

How do teens rage? They starve (*anorexia nervosa*), they vomit (*bulimia nervosa*), they drink, they have sex, they take drugs and they change peer groups.

While it would be easy to misconstrue depression as a simple result of repeatedly disturbed grief processes, the truth is depression can be more complicated. At the root of most depression is grief and loss, but other variables factor in. Genetics, for example, can play a strong role in staking familial propensity for depression onto a teen. Social stresses beyond a teen's emotional capacity to cope may cause depression. Biochemical changes in the brain, such as decreased serotonin, norepinephrine, and dopamine levels, contribute strongly to depression in teens.

In fact, studies have shown that there is an actual biochemical link between the levels of these neurotransmitters and emotions.[50] Festering anger has been shown to decrease the levels of some neurotransmitters within the brain.[51] Lowered neurotransmitters such as norepinephrine or serotonin causes one to feel more depressed and less likely to deal with the anger locked within the heart. Finally, a variety of medical disorders such as hypothyroidism, viral infections, and certain medications can cause depression in teenagers.

My purpose within the scope of this discussion is to simply sketch teen depression in an understandable and workable fashion, with the intent to equip adults to intercede on behalf of teen loved ones and to prevent depression when possible. The good news is that we adults can help our teens a lot more than we think we can.

Periods of Sadness

All teens experience periods of sadness. During these very natural episodes, they may feel confused as to why they are sad. Sadness lasting a week to ten days may be manifested through a lack of interest in being with friends, anger outbursts, or a change in sleep and appetite patterns. Usually these episodes are transient and the teen returns to his or her usual self.

If, however, these episodes persist and last two weeks or longer, the teen may be experiencing depression. Astute physicians screen teenagers for depression by following guidelines provided from the American Psychiatric Association. In the *Diagnostic and Statistical Manual of Mental Disorders,* edition 4 (DSM-IV), the criteria are outlined to aid physicians in uncovering major depressive episodes. The text summarizes the symptoms in the following manner:

Major Depressive Episode

Discriminating features:
1. Depressed mood or loss of interest or pleasure during the same two-week period

Consistent features:
1. Appetite and sleep disturbance
2. Impaired social and academic functioning
3. Absence of using a mood-altering substance
4. Absence of a physical condition that alters mood

Variable features:
1. Irritability
2. Weight loss or weight gain
3. Insomnia or hypersomnia
4. Psychomotor agitation or retardation
5. Fatigue or loss of energy

6. Feelings of worthlessness or inappropriate guilt

7. Impaired concentration and change in school performance

8. Suicidal ideation

9. Diurnal variation with worsening of symptoms in the morning

10. Unexplained somatic complaints

11. Family history of depression

12. Sleep-wake pattern reversal

Another category of depression in teens is known as dysthymia. Essentially, dysthymia is depression that occurs over a longer period of time and is marked by fluctuating feelings of sadness and hopelessness. The criteria for dysthymic depression summarized from the DSM-IV text are the following:

DYSTHMIC DISORDER

Discriminating feature:

1. Dysphoric mood for at least one year

Consistent features:

1. Symptoms not severe enough to diagnose a major depression

2. Absence of a psychotic illness

3. Absence of use of a mood-altering drug

4. Absence of a physiologic, mood-altering condition

5. Impaired social and academic functioning

Variable features:

1. Poor appetite or overeating

2. Insomnia or hypersomnia

3. Low energy or fatigue

4. Low self-esteem

5. Poor concentration or difficulty making decisions

6. Feelings of hopelessness

7. Irritable mood

8. Difficulty getting along with others

9. Unexplained somatic complaints

10. Family history of a depressive disorder

Remember that with teens and children manifestations of the above symptoms can be different than in adults. Dean Parmelee, author of *Child and Adolescent Psychiatry*, elucidates the manifestations of teen depression by the following symptoms:

- ❖ depressed mood with sadness
- ❖ loneliness
- ❖ irritability or hopelessness
- ❖ self-deprecating ideation (feelings of being worthless or stupid)
- ❖ agitation (fighting with peers, disrespect for authority)
- ❖ sleep disturbances (too much or too little)
- ❖ change in school performance (poor concentration)
- ❖ diminished socialization
- ❖ change in attitude toward school
- ❖ somatic (physical) complaints
- ❖ loss of usual energy and change in appetite or weight (becoming a picky or voracious eater when previously normal)[52]

While medical professionals use a number of questions in evaluating depression in teens, I recommend that parents simply begin asking their teens about their feelings in a non-threatening manner. One might ask a son or daughter, "I notice that you're not quite yourself lately. Are you sad a lot?"

Sometimes asking the teen if he is depressed suffices. When kids are feeling blue, sometimes they become very straightforward, wanting help. Researchers have identified potential risk factors for suicide attempts among adolescents. These risk factors include: being female and not living with both parents; psychopathology, including a major depressive disorder; a previous suicide attempt; hopelessness; poor problem-solving abilities and coping skills; impulsivity; a recent stressful life event (including a suicide attempt by family member or friend); family violence and dysfunction; peer difficulties; lower academic achievement; and school problems.[53]

While we can look back upon teens who have attempted suicide and associate these factors, prediction of teens who are at risk for suicide can still be difficult. In 1994 a study assessing risk factors for future suicide attempts found the following predictive factors: a history of a past attempt; current suicidal ideation (or thinking about suicide); a recent attempt by a friend to commit suicide; low self-esteem; and having been born to a teen mother.[54]

In my opinion, nothing replaces the emotional "gestalt" of an attentive parent: mothers knowing their children, fathers knowing their children. Rarely is an involved parent surprised by the announcement of depression as the diagnosis for their troubled teen.

Chapter Fourteen

LOSS OF DEPENDENCE

S IMPLY GROWING INTO PUBERTY TRIGGERS A WELL OF EMOTIONS
for teens. When puberty hits, bodily changes remind them that
life as they once knew it is gone. For many teens, that life
encompassed dependence upon Mom and Dad to make decisions for
them, direct their comings and goings, and bolster them with emotional security and guidance. While outwardly many teens appear
thrilled, their hearts are grieving.

The loss of dependence prompts a realization that now they need
to find deeper emotional resources and begin to make decisions about
homework, athletic events, schedules, likes, and dislikes. Change is
frightening for adolescents. Remember, adults are well-versed in adap-
tation and assuming new direction. Adolescents aren't, and while they
may be intellectually aware that new directions have to be taken, they
are terrified by the prospect.

To further complicate matters, their sadness may manifest itself in
obnoxious behavior that upsets parents. We wonder, *What happened
to that quiet, compliant child?* This triggers a series of emotions within parents that includes disappointment, anger, and sadness. Parents
react either by trying to change the teen back (through increased

demands) or by withdrawing from the teen. The latter reaction makes the teen feel more isolated and hence, even sadder.

All teens experience sadness as they mature beyond the innocent prepubertal years. Angie was one such teen. She and her mother never got along. I remember when I first saw Angie. She came with a litany of physical complaints, convinced that she had cancer or some malady that would kill her soon. After several visits and long conversations, we concluded that her physical ailments were the result of a deeper psychological distress—depression.

Angie began counseling with an excellent therapist who began untangling the friction between her mother and her. For about four months Angie improved and went off to college. Quite honestly her mother was relieved. Angie, without her mother present, confided that she couldn't "wait to get out of the house."

During the first three months of college life, Angie phoned home twice a week, usually in tears with her mother. Shortly after the start of college, she returned home with a major depressive episode that required intense psychotherapy and antidepressant medication.

What happened to Angie? Looking back on her teen years, Angie's high school years reveal that whenever she tried to assert even minimal independence from her mother, her mother reined her in tightly, refusing to extend her curfew beyond 10 p.m. Other times her mother became angry and withdrawn from Angie, which caused the teen to feel confused and angry.

As Angie matured, she felt sad that her relationship with her mother changed. She wanted their relationship to stay the same, and when she saw it change, her reaction triggered fights with her mother.

To complicate matters, her mother perceived that she "needed" Angie to remain dependent upon her. Subconsciously she tried harder to foster Angie's dependence upon her, which caused Angie to act out. Both were "glad" when she finally went off to college. Then an interesting thing happened: at college, Angie's separation from her mother caused her to feel something had been "torn out" of her. Angie had been suddenly ripped from her dependent relationship with her mother, and the natural grieving over that loss of dependence hit her like a ton of bricks.

Angie's first year of college was disastrous, but at the time of this writing, Angie is doing well. Her grieving process resumed and progressed to a conclusion. What were her losses? They were essentially twofold. First, she lost the security of having her mother take care of everything for her. Second, she "lost" an unhealthy relationship with her mother who, in fact, realized that her neediness of Angie was not healthy.

FINDING A BALANCE

Relationships between mothers and daughters can be quite complicated, but those between fathers and daughters can be complicated as well. Either way, finding a healthy balance in parenting our teens is very important, but often seems tough. In fact, we feel as though we can't win.

Conscientious parents toil to find the right balance, allowing separation and independence while gently letting go, offering a safe place for our teens as they recoil back home to dependency. Then we desire them to stretch in situations that afford them the opportunity to find out for themselves how they should think and respond. We want to make decisions for them, but we don't do so. Sometimes we let go too much, other times too little. Will we ever get it right? Fortunately, I believe that if we are strong enough to examine ourselves and our teens, we can come pretty close.

I was privileged to be introduced to Melanie by both of her parents. They brought Melanie, seventeen years old, to see me because, they said, she was "struggling with an eating disorder."

"Oh," I began with Melanie's mother, "what seems to be the problem?"

"She throws up after she eats," her mother replied. "We believe she has *bulimia*."

"Melanie, what do you think? Do you struggle like your parents say?" I traced her posture with a glance.

"I guess so," she responded, looking at my feet.

Her parents chronicled her eating and purging patterns and talked easily about Melanie. Our discussion was unusual. Typically, girls with *bulimia nervosa* work hard to hide their purging. Perhaps her parents had been overly fastidious in observing her behavior. But as our conversation progressed, I realized that indeed she had told them of her behavior.

As Melanie's parents talked about her, they seemed obviously proud of her. Not of her bulimic tendencies, but of her academic accomplishments and her personal discipline amongst the family. She did laundry, kept the house neat, helped care for her younger siblings, earned excellent grades in all of her home-school courses, and was "a great kid."

Melanie was the oldest of six children. When I asked her over the ensuing visits about her family, she described her parents as quiet but open. She held great respect for each of them. She obviously enjoyed telling me of her abilities around the house and her academic performance.

"Have you ever gotten bad grades?" I prodded.

"No. I'm pretty lucky I guess," she responded.

"Have you ever failed at anything? Track, tests, relationships?" I inquired.

"No, not really. I've never failed a test, and I sure don't want to. Relationship—that's a weird question." She sat quietly, wondering if I was an oddball.

"I don't have any friends," she continued. "Janie's thirty years old, and she has bulimia too. I'm really lucky that we can talk about it. She helps me a lot."

When I asked Melanie about other friends, she confided that she really didn't have any close girlfriends her age. In fact, she revealed that she lived a somewhat cloistered existence. Her parents had high expectations for her and feared exposing her to the "real" world. She was home schooled, not permitted to listen to very much music, and rarely allowed to see movies. Her parents' concerns were valid, but Melanie had little input concerning her world. Whenever Melanie voiced her opinion regarding movies, music, school, or friends, her parents responded that their standards were higher than hers. Furthermore, they communicated disappointment regarding her outside activities.

Subsequently Melanie felt that she continually disappointed her parents. She perceived, often correctly, that their love was withdrawn or at least not expressed, which was painful. Melanie continued to pursue activities that evoked her parents' approval. In essence, she jumped through a multitude of hoops to be "the perfect" teen in order to avoid experiencing disapproval because disapproval meant withdrawal of her parents' love.

Unfortunately, like most teens suffering from an eating disorder, her pursuit of perfection never got her what she wanted—a sense that she was lovable regardless of her performance. Melanie became angry because she didn't get what she wanted, so she took it out on herself. She starved, she binged, and she purged.

Clearly her parents needed to learn to communicate their very real love to Melanie. In fact, her parents loved her deeply though they failed to recognize the motivation behind Melanie's pursuit of perfection. Her parents were, in fact, in a powerful position to diffuse the vicious cycle.

Additionally, they needed to recognize her need to move from a dependent posture to an independent one. Melanie was afraid to begin making her own decisions, to think separately, and so were her parents. We parents grieve as we see our teens grow. Loosening the ties makes us feel that we are no longer needed to make decisions for them. We can't always change their immediate environment, but we must transfer skills to teens like Melanie to help them choose healthy relationships and release them from complete dependency on us.

Melanie truly had a love-hate relationship with her parents. She wanted to be dependent upon them to make decisions for her, but staying unnaturally dependent was literally killing her. They had taught her well—she was savvy at choosing movies, music, and friends—but was afraid to do so. Losing dependency is painful, but not losing it, as Melanie's life illustrates, is worse.

OVERPERMISSIVENESS

Overprotectiveness and failing to nurture teens toward independence can trigger depression, but the other extreme—overpermissiveness—can be more harmful. Sadly, this is often the case amongst early adolescents who are victims of divorce.

Greg was ten when his parents split up. He wasn't surprised when it finally happened, he said, because they had been separated for several years. Greg was an only child and revealed to me that he felt quite "lucky" because his parents lived close to one another and he got to see each one fairly frequently.

For financial survival, both parents had to work after the divorce, and every day after school he came home to an empty house—either at Mom's or Dad's. He passed his time playing Nintendo, watching television, or talking on the phone. His mother often had work to do at night, so while at her house, he spent many evenings alone in his room. At his father's house, he said he watched more TV and did all the cooking since his dad was terrible in the kitchen.

As is typical for many children of divorce, Greg hated what the breakup had done to his family. He witnessed his parents withdraw from one another and from him. On some level, he blamed himself for their divorce and fantasized that he could reunite them. When this never happened, he became frustrated. He isolated himself emotionally and began making all of his own decisions about how to spend his free time.

When he chose to go out, his parents gave him carte blanche permission. Movies, music, peers, school work—when and how much to do—he made the decisions. By the time Greg was fifteen, he was drinking, smoking marijuana, and continually getting in trouble at school. He became sexually promiscuous and within a short time, very depressed.

Greg's parents are nice people. They loved him and did the best they could. Unfortunately, reflecting upon Greg's early adolescent years, he was thrust out of a dependent position regarding decision-making. He felt forced to make his own decisions, cognitively as well as emotionally, and he was unable to make healthy ones.

Unfortunately, Greg will have to be "reparented" from a posture of dependency into independence in order to heal his depression. Having appropriate dependence upon parents—at least one—teaches kids they are loved. Remember, kids perceive love differently than adults, and helping them make decisions communicates love and at the same time teaches teens how to set their own parameters regarding friends, free time, etc.

Before we look into the losses our teens face, clarification is in order. First, there are normal, age-appropriate losses that are important transitions necessary for healthy teen development. In fact, the teen years are defined by loss and replacement. Teens lose one body shape and receive another. They let go of concrete thinking patterns in order to utilize more abstract ones. Dependence upon parents for a variety of functions is traded for independence. Some exchanges can be as superficial as change in facial appearance or run as deep as spiritual ones, such as internalizing God as their very own, personal Deity.

Loss during these transitions is ongoing, but there is an extremely important distinguishing characteristic with these healthy age-appropriate losses: they are replaced with something that makes them stronger. Baby fat turns to muscle, dependence gives way to independence, and Dad's God becomes his God.

Because the losses are filled in due order, depression does not ensue. Sadness is felt, to be sure, but a natural resolution to the grieving occurs because something positive is around the next corner.

Depression comes to teens when losses are unnatural, ungrieved, age-inappropriate, or replaced with something destructive. Teens who outgrow their prepubertal identity and fail to grasp a new understanding of their identity become depressed. Teens who harbor anger and hurt over empty losses become depressed because their grief has never rightly concluded.

LOSS OF CONTROL

Severing physical and emotional ties of dependence necessitates a transfer of control from parent to teen. Inherent in the healthy transition is the notion that the teen is gaining capability to make good decisions and then act upon them.

What he decides and believes impacts his behavior. At one time, his parents determined his action, but now his decisions count in a bigger way. The knowledge that he can think intelligently and act responsibly allows his self-esteem to soar.

Parents who fear the decisions their teens will make may become domineering—thus communicating that a teen is not capable of making important decisions on his own. Teens believe parents. If parents see them as capable, chances are good that they will be. If they treat them as incapable, teens will remain incapable.

When teens are taught to make decisions, they are exercising control over themselves. This control feels new and quite powerful. The fact that they can exercise control bolsters their own sense of value as a person.

Control is particularly important for teen girls. If you think about it, the feminist movement was all about control. Women fought for the right to vote, to work outside the home, and to be acknowledged as being independent from males. On many fronts, we women have won and yet we have lost. Teen girls have more choices available today than generations past, and yet, never in the history of our culture, have we experienced such suffrage of the feminine identity and control. Today, date rape is a household word, wives are beaten every day in every town, and sexual abuse of women is estimated between 25 percent to 33 percent nationally.

Teen girls are living in a culture that communicates on a deeper level they may be out of control. Sexually transmitted diseases are epidemic among teen girls. Teen pregnancy remains a national problem, and HIV is certainly infiltrating the community of teen girls. Magazine articles perpetuate claims that female identity increases and decreases with bust size. Why do they do this? Because there is a lot of money to be made by enticing our kids to be sexually active.

We recognize these trends and see that our culture is poisonous to the female teen identity and devastating to the teen perception of who she really is. Our culture defines a teen girl as sexually vulnerable and yet unable to take charge over her thinking and her behavior.

Why do we adults, separate from the media, cast the same thinking onto our own daughters? We perpetuate the communication that she has no choice over her behavior. No choice over pregnancy. No choice over self-image, no choice over drugs, and no choice over sexual promiscuity. Teen girls need to know—each teen girl, one at a time—that they *can* have charge over themselves.

When teen girls experience a sense of lost control, depression often ensues. Remember, gaining charge over one's feelings and behavior is the vital foundation of healthy maturity during the teen years. Losing that sense of control is deeply damaging to emotional maturity.

Conversations with a multitude of depressed teen girls affirms this very phenomenon. One central theme among many girls suffering from anorexia and bulimia is the issue of control. Most have lost a sense of being able to control anything in their world, and they will voraciously attack the closest thing they can control—food. They will starve, or they will eat and purge, but they will take charge.

The problem is, however, that this form of control over food is self-destructive, plummeting girls into a downward spiral of depression. They are taking charge of food for all the wrong reasons; they perceive that they are unable to control other aspects of their lives. Healthy parenting thus means interceding and redirecting them into areas where they can make decisions and take control of behavior in a positive manner.

The great irony with girls suffering from eating disorders is that food ultimately feels like it controls them. Food is huge; they are small. I routinely ask girls with anorexia or bulimia how "big" food feels on a scale of one to ten: one being minuscule, ten being larger than they are. Inevitably, they respond with a "nine" or "ten." As healing progresses, food moves toward a two or one.

Let us think back to some of the teens we have discussed. Remember beautiful Rachel, hemorrhaging from an abortion on an exam table? Was she depressed? Certainly, because she had lost a child (as she described it to me). She had lost her boyfriend, and contrary to what her situation may seem, she had lost a sense of control over her body.

Some might argue that her lifestyle evidenced responsible decision-making. In fact, while sexually active she kept her grades at a respectable level, was close to finishing high school, and looked forward to college. From outward appearances, she looked responsible and in charge. Her belly never swelled with a pregnancy and she didn't lose many school days.

I submit, however, that those of us who perceive that Rachel was indeed in control are seriously misguided. That day on my exam table,

I watched a teen scream, and I can assure you that she had deeply lost control of her body, her emotions, and her self. Amidst the losses, there were no replacements. Unfortunately for Rachel, as she left my office she greeted a culture that encouraged her to lose more by having sex with others.

And then there was Ellen, so assertive and driven, commanding in presence, yet she suffered depression from age-inappropriate losses that were unfilled and ungrieved. First, she lost a profound sense of control over her body when she was sexually abused as a child. That event showered her with shame and fear. It sexualized her feelings, which led her to associate her desire for touch and love with sexual activity. Thus, whenever she desired healthy love or touch, she acted out sexually with boyfriends.

She started early at fourteen because of a deep subconscious need for attention. The problem was not Ellen but her culture. Outwardly, she looked like just another curious and healthy teen who decided to be sexually active. Her culture provided a smooth avenue for her pain to go unnoticed. Her losses of dignity and broken sexuality easily meshed into "normal" adolescent behavior and consequently became more painful. Ellen's losses led her into deep depression.

To compound matters, the pain from her sexual abuse worsened each time she was sexually active. This is what young men and women lose when they lose their virginity: self-respect, the knowledge that they can control their bodies, physical health (when all-too-frequent STDs ensue), trust (if the relationship dissolves—which it usually does), and even hope since many believe subconsciously that sex will bring happiness or contentment.

SEXUAL ACTIVITY AND DEPRESSION

Studies have shown that the earlier teens start having sex, the more partners they will have.[55] Many adults hold the belief that teens are sexually active because they have healthy sexual drives. Sexual experimentation, they conclude, can therefore be a healthy part of the teen years. My experience with teens leads me to strongly disagree. Sexual activity during the teen years invites depression into the lives of teens. Why would this be?

Consider the losses incurred during the sexual encounter. Some of the losses occur on the conscious level, but *most occur on the subconscious level.*

First, there is the surrendering of deeply personal boundaries when teens engage in sex. They often feel painfully vulnerable after breaching their boundaries, losing elements of self-respect, privacy, and self-protection.

Second, they lose control because they allow their intense emotions (infatuation) and physical urges (lust) to overtake them. This loss of control feels exciting in the heat of the moment, but afterward proves very frightening.

Third, the sexual relationship breaks down trust and honesty between them and their parents—even their siblings or closest friends. Part of them may want to hide from those whom they respect. And yet to others whom they respect less (we're talking about boys here), they may try to boast about their masculine prowess. From my viewpoint, the bravado exists to hide deep disappointment and low self-esteem.

Fourth, and most important, is the *loss of hope.* All teens desire deeper intimacy, self-respect, love, and safety. For a fleeting moment during their sexual encounters, they may experience fulfillment of one or all of these needs, but in the end, they become frustrated and disappointed. Why? Let's look at the reasons in detail.

Teens enter sexual encounters hoping that the event will satisfy (at least in part) their very real and healthy needs for intimacy. For love. For a deeper sense of value and safety. When satiety comes only superficially, they feel confused, hurt, and frustrated.

The sexual encounter plays a cruel game on teens. It provides enough titillation and comfort to seduce teens into believing that it will satisfy their needs. The problem is, however, that it doesn't—at least in any meaningful or substantive way—because what they experienced did not meet their deep emotional needs.

Since teens do not have the maturity to understand this, they often go back to sex, trying again to get what they need. Each time they return, the experience of having their needs left unsatisfied by sex leaves them more frustrated, more disappointed. The problem isn't what they need, the problem is that they are simply looking in the wrong place—but they don't know this.

All teens do know is that they feel hurt and confused. Further they feel that since the problem isn't with sex (everything around them says it's great), the problem must lie within themselves. And here's the real blow. That problem within themselves is their needs. Thus, they learn to ignore their needs and give up hope that they can be met. And when they give up hope, their hearts grow cold and numb.

This development leaves teens ripe for depression. Remember: depression sets in when losses accumulate in the heart and are left unrecognized and unresolved. Teens can enter depression precisely because the losses they experience through sex are wholly unrecognized by the teens themselves. What I've noticed is that when teens feel disappointed or confused after a sexual encounter, they refrain from telling anyone lest they admit to their parents they had sex. Or they resist explaining their frustrations to their peers because they don't want to risk looking like a geek. Hiding their hurts, these teens allow them to fester deep within their hearts, like an infected abscess.

The above dissection of emotional events is a simplification of what happens in many teens' hearts. If we factor in a history of sexual abuse (which affects between one in three to one in four girls), pain from a broken family, chronic illness, poor grades, and alcohol or drug use, the entire chain of emotional events is more convoluted and more severe.

Sex is not for kids because it puts them at risk for more than pregnancy, infertility, and sexually transmitted diseases: it fractures their hearts and souls. And no one will acknowledge this.

Chapter Fifteen

A HOPE OF CONTROL

REMEMBER MICHAEL IN CHAPTER 3? HE RAN TRACK, WORKED at a restaurant, and struggled about leaving Adrianna. He agonized over decisions regarding sexual involvement, but he took charge of his life in a healthy manner. He thought through his decisions carefully, then decided to wait to have sex with someone he loved. Believing that he could make decisions gave him a deep sense of control and a rich sense of who he was as a young man. No one was in charge of his body but himself.

Unfortunately, many young men—and young women—feel like Michael in our culture. Teens see their sexuality being defined through the media, advertisements, and music. It is not a flattering sexuality, but one that diminishes their worth. "Cheap sex" is damaging and cruel to young people, giving them a sense that they are not expected to have control over their bodies sexually. This perceived expectation of loss of control hurts them mentally and emotionally as well, opening clear passage for potential depression.

Rachel didn't need a shot of Depoprovera to ward off another pregnancy. She needed a mature woman who would embrace her and invest in her. Without intercession, Rachel's depression and loss of control spiraled out of hand.

LOSS OF INTIMACY

When kids are little, they are adorable. We touch toddlers, throw them up over our heads, swirl them, and snuggle them onto our laps. We comb their hair, help them dress, and bathe them. Quite appropriately, as puberty approaches we retreat physically, allowing them to care for their physical needs. Sadly, though, we stop touching them. Perhaps we are uncomfortable with their maturing bodies. Perhaps we wonder: How do we touch? When do we touch? We are unsure, so we retreat and cease touching.

Teens lose physical intimacy with their parents, and part of them is relieved. But there is another part that grieves what once was. Few teens can articulate it, but being small meant being touched, being seen, and being loved. Being a teenager means being left alone and loved less. With the maturing of the body comes less touch by parents.

Adults, remember, will not make this jump in thinking because we are equipped with more sophisticated cognition. But young teens often harbor concrete thinking that allows jumps to be made: *I am not touched, so I am not loved.* Crazy, we think, but we are not teens.

Teens need intimacy so they search for a place to share. *Where will my thoughts and feelings land safely?* Peers present such safety, so they try them out. Healthy friendship can provide a wonderful outlet for intimacy needs. Friends can offer a platform from which teens can test more sophisticated thoughts and greater complexity of feelings. Friendships can provide an opportunity for vulnerability that can be a positive and strengthening experience.

If, however, teens land in a peer group populated with hurting teens, the experience of intimacy can be destructive. For instance, if a teen opens himself and doesn't find acceptance, he will assume that something is wrong with him. His need for intimacy is so strong that he will change whatever he can in his personality, appearance, and sense of humor to find acceptance. Peer groups with hurting teens are not safe places; they are pressure cookers.

This is why gangs are a hotbed of rejection, broken intimacy, and shame. Members have not found acceptance or intimacy anywhere, which makes them willing to adapt their behavior into some semblance of acceptability with the gang. To teens, power is attractive. Power translates into bullying, hurting, and domineering. Dominance to a teen gang member serves two purposes: it affords him acceptance (since power is attractive) and it affords him an escape valve for his rage.

STIRRING A DEEP WONDERING

Teens have a problem with intimacy because their needs are so great they will search a host of relationships until they find it. If they don't find the real thing, they will accept a cheap substitute.

Failure to experience intimacy leads to isolation and loneliness, two of the most intolerable of human emotions. Loneliness stirs a deep wondering: "Am I not worthy of anyone's company? Am I unlovable?"

Loneliness is devastating and costs our country millions, perhaps billions, each year. High teen pregnancy rates, sexual activity, gang violence, and drug use are cries of youth in desperate search for any behavior dissipating loneliness. Loneliness also drives sexual behavior. Parents know this, physicians know it, but we continue to approach our teens with the idea that "education" will keep them out of bed. Tell them more, teach them more.

What they don't need is more education or condoms but intimacy and connection. I fear that if we fail to tackle this most fundamental of human needs from the ground up, we will continue to see an escalation of gang-related crime, depression, and other assortments of teen ills. We adults are in a remarkably sound position to intervene, even if we, too, suffer from loneliness.

This is what I observe among sexually active teens. Typically a teen girl avails herself to a boy, allowing him to literally see who she is.

She opens up, he takes, and she hopes something deeper will happen. They connect emotionally. She likes it, he likes it, and satisfaction ensues. But it's never long lasting. He eventually leaves, and she assumes that something is wrong with her. She grieves her primary loss of intimacy, which leads her to a secondary one. When the pattern repeats itself, she feels worse, tries again with a new partner, and finds herself in an emotional state of escalating depression.

Condoms are not the answer for her. Intimacy is. She needs to know that she is a marvelous young woman worthy of attention, and that sex will never be the answer.

LOSS OF SELF-WORTH

There has been no more confusing time in the history of the American culture than the start of this new millennium. Teen girls are not immune to pressure from media images, so let us not be fooled. Our girls are taught that they can be intelligent, financially independent, and emotionally and physically capable of creating a lifestyle in which they are dependent upon no one—least of all another man or husband. They can have children and the government will take care of them.

Young men on the other hand, are defined by what they are *not* supposed to be. They should not be the sole providers of financial security in a home, domineering, insensitive, or aggressive. Traditional roles of emerging maleness have fractured, and teen men are adrift, wondering where to go and how to be male. Some of the changes facing teens about their value are good, but many are mind-boggling.

Teen girls and boys are confused. We parents are confused as to how to teach them about their gender identity and their value. They perceive that their value exists as a balanced combination of three factors:

1. What they look like

2. How much they perform (capability)

3. What others think of them (lovability)

Generally, if a teen feels that all three factors are positive in his life, then he is valuable. A teen may believe, "If I get good grades, I am smart. If I am smart, others will like me. If others like me, then I am valuable."

As teens' interests broaden, they may try different ventures. For instance, Addie loved figure skating. By sixteen, she was a brilliant and accomplished artist on the ice. Her parents supported her expensive skating lessons, believing that the sport was good for her.

Addie practiced long hours before and after school—until she hit junior year when Addie stopped skating. She was burned out; she hated practicing triple jumps. While her parents were disappointed, they embraced her decision and supported the change. Over the ensuing two years, Addie tried everything from drama to music to art: testing, changing, failing, restarting. Each time she "failed," she learned an invaluable lesson from her parents, who communicated to her that she was no less lovable. Addie's parents didn't "need" her to excel, they simply loved her.

Addie, while struggling to figure out how and where she "fit" into the adult world, thrived and emerged with a keener sense of herself as a strong young woman. So why did Addie keep jumping from interest to interest?

First, she was testing her capability, but more importantly, she was testing exactly what part her performance played in her deeper sense of self. Finally, she needed to know how significant her performance was to those she loved. Addie grew to realize that she was capable of athletic achievement because she was highly disciplined and talented in this area. This made her feel good about herself. When she left ice skating, she initially felt that she "failed," but she endured and was able to like herself. She received love by her family and close friends.

In short, performance no longer held Addie captive. Often teens are driven to perform and please others because it bolsters their sense of value. We parents perpetuate this drive because we applaud good performances, but Addie's parents gave her the freedom to try new things.

Teen boys who test the limits and scope of their capability are met with strong messages from their culture. They hear messages like: you are domineering (as music and movies portray), you are sexual (you gotta have it), and you are more male if you can combine the two. Young men pick up on these cues and exercise dominance and sexual acting out, which may indeed help them "feel" more capable.

Unfortunately, as with the source for intimacy, the temporary realization of male identity as domineering and sexual is unsatisfying. For as they embrace these characteristics, they find that being dominant does not enhance their sense of capability.

Contrary to popular thinking, teen boys hurt during sexual encounters. They are not emotionless, out-of-control packages of human flesh. They are young men in deep need of lovability. Sexual activity affords them an opportunity to test this out, but as with teen girls, it doesn't work. They discover that even when they are "successful" in the most banal of performances, they are still left hurting and empty. They try again in search of affirmation. They don't find it, and the sense of loss and grief deepens, which causes depression to ensue.

BEST FRIENDS

In 1987, Elayne Bennett decided to help teen girls who didn't have the maturity to either articulate their struggles or withstand peer pressure by themselves. She began the Best Friends program in Washington, D.C., for girls in grades 5 through 12 from a cross section of socioeconomic planes.

Mrs. Bennett recruited volunteer women to aid these girls in character building by fostering "self-respect through self-restraint." Best

Friends offers role modeling, mentoring, fitness classes, and cultural and public services for teen girls. Quite simply, adult women intervene in the lives of willing teen girls with these simple messages:

❖ You are special and worth preserving

❖ You are capable of making healthy decisions

❖ You are lovable just where you are

These women went into area schools and asked for young girls to participate in this "preservation program." Girls responded and liked being set apart. They committed to one another to remain in control of their lives by being sexually pure. With the help of adult women who believed in them, teen girls weathered the years of identity crisis in a positive and healthy environment. No cheap substitutes for intimacy or identity were accepted.

What has come out of the Best Friends program? Mrs. Bennett points to decreased pregnancy rates and an escalating sense of worth amongst the teen participants within the suburbs of Washington, D.C. An independent 1995 evaluation revealed the following outcomes for the Best Friends girls:

❖ 5 percent of Best Friends girls were sexually active, compared to 63 percent of peers attending D.C. public schools.

❖ 1 percent of Best Friends girls became pregnant before high school graduation, compared to 20 percent (with 6 percent for the second time) of fellow students in D.C. schools.[56]

The messages and principles of the program are profoundly simple. Best Friends helps teen girls see that they are facing inordinate pressures at a time when they feel their identity is up for grabs. Further, Best Friends helps them reject notions that their worth is significantly linked to their looks or their sexual activity. In an atmosphere replete with acceptance amongst peers and adult women, teen girls thrive.

Thriving is what it is all about. Hope for teens begins with hope from a parent or concerned friend.

Chapter Sixteen

HOPE FOR PARENTS
IS HOPE FOR TEENS

When Kate learned that hospitalization was imminent
She crept onto her father's lap with reptilian
precision and curled her five-and-a-half foot frame into
a perfect ball.
When his arms encircled her frame,
her healing began.

A CULTURAL TREND HAS EVOLVED THAT IS DISTURBING TO family dynamics and ultimately our children's health. This trend is the evisceration of parental influence and authority. Why has this happened? The reasons are multifaceted. We see parents projected in Hollywood films as bumbling idiots. We see parents contend with the pain of divorce and separation from their children. We see guilt over broken marriages, exhaustive work schedules, and bimonthly visits that spin parents into a vortex of confusion regarding how much impact, if any, they really have on their kids' lives.

When we hear that parents may not have that much influence, however, some of us feel relieved because we are absolved from responsibility if our children's lives go awry. "Well," we surmise, "since he's his own person, there's not much we could have done anyway."

Certainly a teen is his own person, born with unique characteristics and a personality style unlike any other human. While a parent cannot alter the fundamental "wiring" of a child, a father or mother can certainly crush or uplift the spirit. The latter is done by meeting his deep needs.

There exists a tension surrounding parental influence. For instance, teens with Attention Deficit Hyperactivity Disorder (ADHD) are chemically and behaviorally different than their peers. While their parents can't take ADHD away, parents most certainly can provide behavior modification teaching and predictability in the teen's environment, in addition to finding good medical care and proper medication.

My personal experience with ADHD children is that parents quickly lose confidence because they don't see immediate results from their efforts in trying to influence or modify their child's behavior or they buy into the notion that "we just can't do anything anyway." But if parents believe that they have a powerful chance to change the behavior of their teen (not the presence of his ADHD) and learn to look for behavior changes over years instead of days, their parenting becomes more effective.

HEALTHY PARENTS, HEALTHY TEENS

Why is it imperative for parents to recognize their power in a teen's life? First, because it is true and is evidenced throughout medical, educational, and psychiatric literature. Second, because if parents are emotionally healthy, then teens are likely to be healthy.

Time and again teachers tell me they can write the scenario of their students' home life simply by watching the teens in their classroom. Our children's tone of voice, the fashions they wear, and their behavior speak volumes about the emotional health (or lack thereof) of the children's parents. This is unnerving but true. Hope for emotionally healthy and mature teens begins with healthy parents.

Research shows that what adults believe about kids influences them—in positive and negative ways. I have selected one of the best studies in education to support this statement. Robert Rosenthal and Lenore Jacobs wrote a book called *Pygmalion in the Classroom*. They describe their research on teachers and students by stating the following: "The central idea of this book has been that one person's expectations for another's behavior could come to serve as a self-fulfilling prophesy."[57] Thus, they determined to investigate how a student's achievements were affected by the beliefs of that student's teacher.

They selected Oak School, an elementary school drawing from a lower-class community in a medium-sized city, to complete their research. Each child in the school was tested with a standard nonverbal test of intelligence at the start of the study. The test showed total IQ, verbal IQ, and reasoning IQ.

After completing the testing, eighteen teachers were informed that certain children received scores that showed exceptional potential. The teachers were told who these children were and that the children were expected to show "dramatic intellectual growth." About 20 percent of Oak School's children were identified as these special children.

In fact, these children *did not* have exceptional scores and were selected at random. Rosenthal states, "The difference between the special children and the ordinary children, then, was only in the mind of the teacher."[58]

The school year continued, and the children were retested at the end of one semester, at the end of the school year, and then after two years. The results? Twenty percent of the children who were not identified to the teachers as having exceptional potential (the control group) saw their IQ scores rise twenty or more points. In the "selected" group of kids, however, 47 percent showed a rise of twenty or more IQ points.[59]

What happened? Remember, the only difference between the control group and the selected group was the beliefs of their teachers. When the teachers *believed* that their students were capable of superior work, the students responded. What these significant adults believed was communicated to the children, who internalized those feelings and acted upon them.

If teachers can influence children so profoundly, is it not reasonable to assume that you have equal or greater influence over your children? Certainly. With teachers, the relationship with students has fewer complications than those experienced in parent/child relationships. You have more influence because the depth of the relationships with your children is greater. You have the ability to elevate or crush a child's belief about himself.

Let's review some common misbeliefs that parents often have about their teens. There are four myths parents often espouse that can be toxic to parent-teen relationships.

1. My teen doesn't really need me.

Hopefully after reading about the needs of teens and their cognitive limitations, you can understand how fundamentally wrong this notion is. Teens need adults and parents to stay physically and emotionally alive. Unfortunately in our fast-paced, let's-grow-kids-up-as-fast-as-we-can culture, we are seduced into thinking that our teens are more mature than they really are.

We parents are influenced by our own peers racing to have our kids outdistance and outperform our friends' kids. We overschedule our kids because we think that is what we have to do. We think our kids have arrived when they reach high school. They drive. They have boyfriends and girlfriends. They earn good money, balance their new checkbooks, and look forward to college.

Wrong. They look grown up on the outside, but within each teen swirls an entanglement of emotions and ideas, asking who he is and where he fits. Separation anxiety forgotten from his toddler years resurfaces, and he draws on the health or ill-health of his emotional state.

What does he find when he draws from his emotional state of soundness or lack thereof? He finds deep within himself two holes: the "mommy hole" and the "daddy hole." These terms are dubbed in childlike language because the holes were first formed when he was an infant. What are these holes? They are basic needs for mom and for dad. He was born with these two holes or needs, each carved with a specific structure intended to be filled with one (mother or father) whose structure complements his.

St. Augustine said that all humans were born with a God-shaped hole in their hearts that can only be filled by God himself. So, too, is the state of the child's heart with his parents. There exists a mommy-shaped hole and a daddy-shaped hole ready to be filled by these two people.

Before I lose any readers who are foster parents, adoptive parents, or perhaps grandparents raising their grandchildren, let me say that any loving adult can fill these holes when the biological mother or father is unavailable.

How does the teen know if that hole has been filled? He knows by intuition. He recognizes the fullness of love in his relationship with his mother or father, which gives him strength and sense of identity. If the hole is only partially filled, he feels the need to stay, go back, and try again to receive love from Mom or Dad. Broken teens and abandoned teens have empty holes and will try whatever their immature minds conceive to get those holes filled. But even in the most well-adjusted teen the hole is never completely filled. He always needs Mom and Dad's approval and love.

2.　My teen doesn't love me.

Much teen behavior communicates anything but love to the observant eye of a wounded parent. Teens pout, act obnoxious, and try to convince the world that they not only don't love you, but they don't need you, either.

Parents who feel that their teens don't love them anymore have lost their sense of objectivity. This can occur as a result of entangled and wounded feelings. We often believe the hurtful things our teens say. When we believe their comments, we take them personally, immediately finding fault with our parenting by asking ourselves what we did wrong.

In many cases, we've done nothing wrong except believe the crazy things our teens tell us in fits of anger. Most parents wouldn't berate themselves if their two-year-old called them a horrible parent. Why then do we believe our seventeen-year-old when he casts critical slander on our parenting decisions? How does he know what is good parenting and what isn't?

Teens need to love you and receive your love. They don't always know how to show it, unfortunately, and they often try to hide their needs because it makes them feel uncomfortable and dependent. Know that they need to be loved, but also know they don't know how to love and must be taught. Model a better way to them. Realize that their lack of expression of love is out of ignorance and confusion, not out of lack of existence.

3.　Peers are more important than the parents.

All parents know the painful transition in their relationship with their children when suddenly the tender preadolescent who loved to be at home Friday nights now screams about being "forced" to go on family vacations. Time with peers becomes a priority, and this is natural. Parents, however, make a dangerous leap. They perceive peers having a greater influence on their teens than they do.

In the short term, this may be true since teens pattern their behavior after a certain peer group by dressing like them, talking like them, etc. But ultimately, the parent's influence imbeds itself within the heart. It lasts forever, precisely because genuine love, hurt, disappointment, and joy are felt between a parent and a child. Peer relationships are safer and less influential because they are shallower.

Parents who are confused about peer influence versus their own turn their teen loose too easily with peers. We let peers dominate our teen's time and order their weekend and after-school activities because we feel our teens need this. They do need time with peers (healthy peers, of course), but they still need time with parents precisely because our influence is lifelong and peer influence isn't.

Could it be that we turn our teens over to peers too frequently because we'd really rather not deal with them? Or is it because we just don't want one more argument about how much time they're spending away?

Perhaps if we parents recognize that our teens need our influence more than peer influence, we will incorporate more time with them. Teens don't need to like it, but if they learn to expect that a certain portion of their time is allotted for friends and a certain portion is allotted for the family, they will come to accept it.

4.   There's nothing I can do to influence my teen's behavior.

Parents who believe this myth have surrendered their rightful authority, which causes them to feel helpless, frightened and upset. Parents most certainly can influence their teens. As we read earlier, what parents believe about their teens can either positively or negatively affect teen behavior.

In addition, parents can and should make consequences for a teen's bad behaviors. Teens need firm boundaries even more than toddlers need them, although toddlers see how many creative ways they can hurt themselves. Stick a finger in an outlet—she'll try it. How about a thick blue crayon in his nostril (I've pulled more than a couple out!).

Teens can hurt themselves in bigger ways. Just remind yourself of that when you hand them a set of car keys. Three-sixties in icy parking lots prove too tempting to pass by. Opportunities to tread the thrilling line between life and death crop up weekly for the exuberant teen who believes he'll never die. Boundaries can literally save a teen's life.

Many parents surrender their authority over teens because they are confused about whether they should exercise it in the relationship. Rarely is a parent portrayed by the media culture as an intelligent, loving, and authoritative figure. Consider the typical parent appearing in movies and sitcoms. We see them alongside a "cute" adolescent child who cleverly "teaches" his parent a few things about life. Dad is the butt of many teen jokes, and Mom is seen as self-centered or just plain ditzy.

Think of the last time you saw a movie or TV show that portrayed a solid, mature parent giving guidance and a receptive ear to his teen son or daughter? Teens receive an influx of messages from peers and media that parents "can't do anything for them or to them."

But this is their perception and Hollywood's deception. It shouldn't be a healthy parent's, and it certainly isn't the truth. Teens need authority and need their parents to believe in their authority, which creates security. I cannot express this too emphatically.

One mother recently sighed that her sixteen-year-old daughter told her that she was going with some friends to a nearby city to shop, see a show, and spend the night with a friend. The mother told her daughter that she wouldn't allow her to go for a variety of reasons. The daughter then replied that it didn't matter: she was taking her car and going anyway.

The mother told me, "What could I do? She has her own car."

I asked my patient's mother why she didn't simply confiscate the car keys.

"Well," she replied "it's her car."

This teen's mother willingly surrendered her parental authority under the guise of being a loving mother. Her daughter wanted a car, so she let Mom help pay for one. Thus, the daughter concluded, the car was hers. Mistake number one. As long as the daughter lives with her mother and father, they maintain control of the car.

Why? Because the daughter is still under their authority and so is her car. This mother didn't want to get on the "bad" side of her daughter, so she let this young girl keep the car keys and go. Mistake number two. Mom had an opportunity to offer this girl something far more important than a weekend trip. She threw away the chance to stand up to her daughter and teach her that she is living with parents who are willing to fight to protect her.

Not only that, her daughter has to learn that she lives in a world where she can't always have her way. Believe it or not, teens feel very secure when they know they can't act on their whims any time they want. Such knowledge brings great relief.

Those who parent teens with the mindset that there's "nothing they can do" about their teen's behavior have given up on themselves and their teens. Ultimately, it is the teen who loses.

Chapter Seventeen

WHAT WE BELIEVE MATTERS

The best lack all conviction, while the worst
Are full of passionate intensity.

W.B. YEATS

LAST CHAPTER, I CITED A ROSENTHAL AND JACOBS STUDY GIVING solid evidence that adult beliefs can change a child's behavior. How is it that teens know what an adult believes? In some manner, beliefs must be expressed by the adult either by tone of voice, facial expression, body language, or verbal statement. Some form of communication of our beliefs occurs to our kids, often unknowingly.

What we believe matters, and what we express changes our teens' lives. The medical community witnessed these truths with the release of a significant 1997 study of adolescents in the *Journal of the American Medical Association (JAMA)*.

This Add Health Study set out to identify which factors in an adolescent's environment protect him from emotional distress, suicide, violence, substance abuse, and engaging in sexual activity—otherwise known as "high risk" behaviors amongst teens.

The magnitude and scope of this study was unprecedented. Approximately 90,000 teens were studied, and the data was collected meticulously. The *JAMA* report revealed very positive information regarding the influence of parents, noting that when the data was analyzed, the effects of the following variables were controlled for: gender, race, ethnic background, family structure (whether a parent was married or single), and economic level.

What did the study find out regarding which factors protected teens from harmful behavior? First, the study showed that regardless of socioeconomic level or family structure, the role of parents consistently remained at the top of positive influences in teens' lives. "While not surprising, the protective role that perceived parental expectations play emerges as an important recurring correlate of health and healthy behavior," said the report.[60]

This finding supports the work of Rosenthal and Jacobs regarding the impact that parents have on changing the behaviors of their children. The *JAMA* study showed that if adolescents perceive that their parents disapproved of them being sexually active, those adolescents were less likely to engage in that behavior. Parent disapproval served to protect teens with regard to beginning sexual activity. In other words, if a teen believed that his parents disapproved of him being sexually active, he was less likely to become sexually active!

How else did parents impact teen behavior? Very importantly, the study cites "parent connectedness" to teens as one of the highest protections against harmful behaviors. "While physical presence of a parent in the home at key times reduces the risk, it is consistently less significant than parental connectedness (e.g. feelings of warmth, love, and caring from parents)," said the report.[61]

In a culture of harried parents and split families, these statistics can be either frightening or comforting. They reaffirm to parental instincts what we knew in our hearts: parents and family matter in the lives of teens. Research proves it. Parents, regardless of income level, marital status, ethnic background, or race profoundly affect their teens' hearts, minds, and behaviors.

FUNDAMENTAL VALUES

What exactly is parent-family connectedness? The Add Health researchers defined it as the "highest degree of closeness, caring, and satisfaction with parental relationship, whether resident or non-resident mother or father; feeling understood, loved, wanted, and paid attention to by family members."[62]

Could this mean that teens who experience the meeting of their fundamental needs of love and intimacy with a parent experience less emotional distress and are more likely to avoid drugs, alcohol, sexual activity, and violence? The study isn't so specific, but I will be. Parents who meet the fundamental needs of teens *will* have a greater chance of their teens coming out all right.

It is also important to look at the other protective factors in the study, which were school environment and the individual characteristics of teens (self-esteem, paid work outside of school, getting along with others, etc.).

While parent-family connectedness emerged at the top of the list for teens, it is important to note that a sense of connectedness to their school, healthy self-esteem, and grade-point average were also important in keeping teens out of trouble.

Finally, the study found that parental presence during key times of the day was another protective factor for teens regarding involvement in violence, substance abuse, and level of emotional distress. Sadly, because of many economic or cultural demands, teens spend significantly less time with parents (less than ten hours per week) than thirty years ago.

Teens need parents. They need them at home at certain times, and

FORTY DEVELOPMENTAL ASSETS

ASSET TYPE	ASSET NAME AND DEFINITION

Support	1.	**Family Support**—family life provides high levels of love and support.
	2.	**Positive family communication**—young person and her or his parent(s) communicate positively, and young person is willing to seek advice and counsel from parent(s).
	3.	**Other adult relationships**—young person receives support from three or more nonparent adults.
	4.	**Caring neighborhood**—young person experiences caring neighbors.
	5.	**Caring school climate**—school provides a caring, encouraging environment.
	6.	**Parent involvement in schooling**—parent(s) are actively involved in helping young person succeed in school.
Empowerment	7.	**Community values youth**—young person perceives that adults in the community value youth.
	8.	**Youth as resources**—young people are given useful roles in the community.
	9.	**Service to others**—young person serves in the community one hour or more per week.
	10.	**Safety**—young person feels safe at home, school, and in the neighborhood.
Boundaries and Expectations	11.	**Family boundaries**—family has clear rules and consequences and monitors the young person's whereabouts.
	12.	**School boundaries**—school provides clear rules and consequences.
	13.	**Neighborhood boundaries**—neighbors take responsibility for monitoring young people's behavior.
	14.	**Adult role models**—parent(s) and other adults model positive, responsible behavior.
	15.	**Positive peer influence**—young person's best friends model responsible behavior.
	16.	**High expectations**—both parent(s) and teachers encourage the young person to do well.
Constructive Use of Time	17.	**Creative activities**—young person spends three or more hours per week in lessons or practice in music, theater, or other arts.
	18.	**Youth programs**—young person spends three or more hours per week in sports, clubs, or organizations at school and/or in the community.
	19.	**Religious community**—young person spends one or more hours per week in activities in a religious institution.
	20.	**Time at home**—young person is out with friends "with nothing special to do" two or fewer nights per week.

EXTERNAL ASSETS

FORTY DEVELOPMENTAL ASSETS

ASSET TYPE	ASSET NAME AND DEFINITION
Commitment to Learning	21. **Achievement motivation**—young person is motivated to do well in school.
	22. **School engagement**—young person is actively engaged in learning.
	23. **Homework**—young person reports doing at least one hour of homework every school day.
	24. **Bonding to school**—young person cares about his or her school.
	25. **Reading for pleasure**—young person reads for pleasure three or more hours per week.
Positive Values	26. **Caring**—young person places high value on helping other people.
	27. **Equality and social justice**—young person places high value on promoting equality and reducing hunger and poverty.
	28. **Integrity**—young person acts on convictions and stands up for his or her beliefs.
	29. **Honesty**—young person "tells the truth even when it is not easy."
	30. **Responsibility**—young person accepts and takes personal responsibility.
	31. **Restraint**—young person believes it is important not to be sexually active or to use alcohol or other drugs.
Social Competencies	32. **Planning and decision making**—young person knows how to plan ahead and make choices.
	33. **Interpersonal competency**—young person has empathy, sensitivity, and friendship skills.
	34. **Cultural competence**—young person has knowledge of and comfort with people of different cultural/racial/ethnic backgrounds.
	35. **Resistance skills**—young person can resist negative peer pressure and dangerous situations.
	36. **Peaceful conflict resolution**—young person seeks to resolve conflict nonviolently.
Positive Identity	37. **Personal power**—young person feels he or she has control over "things that happen to me."
	38. **Self-esteem**—young person reports having a high self-esteem.
	39. **Sense of purpose**—young person reports that "my life has a purpose."
	40. **Positive view of personal future**—young person is optimistic about her or his personal future.

INTERNAL ASSETS

they are healthier when they perceive love and security at home. We must not be tempted to assume that because their bodies have matured, they need us less. They need us differently.

The Search Institute in Minneapolis, Minnesota, has studied teens and what kids need to be successful in life. Their research led them to compile a list of assets that they identified as integral to healthy development. The Search Institute surveyed almost 100,000 sixth-through ninth-grade students across the United States. Half of the assets they identified are labeled as "external" assets, and half are "internal" assets. These assets, forty in all, are listed in the chart on pages 154 and 155.

Interestingly, seven of the external assets (assets 1-20) directly relate to parental involvement, and almost all of the internal assets can be directly or indirectly influenced by parents.

Family support, positive family communication, parental involvement in school, safety (feeling safe), family boundaries, adult role models, high expectations, and time at home appear in the first twenty assets needed for successful development.

Notice too, under the next category of internal assets, those which parents can affect:

- ❖ achievement motivation (parent's belief that child can do well)
- ❖ caring
- ❖ equality and social justice (reflecting attitudes witnessed at home)
- ❖ integrity
- ❖ honesty
- ❖ responsibility
- ❖ restraint
- ❖ planning and decision-making
- ❖ interpersonal competence
- ❖ resistance skills

- ❖ peaceful conflict resolution
- ❖ self-esteem
- ❖ sense of purpose
- ❖ positive view of personal future

The Search Institute has concluded from their research that the more assets kids have, the more successful in life they will be. "Ideally, all youth would experience at least thirty-one of these forty assets. Yet only 8 percent of youth experience this level of assets, and 62 percent experience fewer than twenty of the assets," said the report.

If existence of a high number of these assets has been shown to protect teens from harmful behaviors, strong parents must be willing to ask themselves, "What am I doing to help build these in my teen's life?"

If the above-cited information can serve any purpose, let it be this: whatever your fears, marital status, or insecurities, be convinced that your teen needs you. There is a hole in their hearts waiting to be filled by you. If you choose to fill it, your teens will not search elsewhere to have it filled. Do it now. Roll up your sleeves and for the sake of their emotional, intellectual, and physical health, begin wherever you can to meet their fundamental needs.

They need your intervention, regardless of how tentative you feel. Be assured that contrary to what you may witness in their behavior at home, they want your genuine involvement. Let's see how we can give all of our teens what they really need from us.

Chapter Eighteen

HELP FOR PARENTS EQUALS HELP FOR TEENS

MOTHER TERESA WILL BE RECORDED IN HISTORY AS A MODEL of peace in a broken world. How did this tiny woman, so humble and unassuming, impact the entire globe? Was it her intellect and drive? Certainly not. Most of us don't know anything about her educational status, but what we do know is her heart. Many believe the real mystery of her success was God-alive in the work of her life and tiny hands. Mother Teresa loved God, served His people, and touched the despised.

Many of us could not choose her life of poverty or could not touch those with communicable diseases. We will give money to worthy causes, but don't ask us to touch diseased people. Yet that is what physical intimacy is all about.

PHYSICAL INTIMACY

Physical touch requires connection. My flesh and your flesh. Touch between humans is unnerving and awkward for most of us. We even have difficulty saying what it produces—intimacy. What will the other person learn about us? So we are uncomfortable, nervous, and shy. Yet if we don't touch others, they won't learn these things about us.

Mother Teresa was not afraid of what others would see in her. Interestingly, photos show her frequently touching people—one at a time—on the face. The face is the most intimate place to be touched because it involves eye contact. I don't think she cared because Mother Teresa realized the power of healing with the touch of her tiny hands. Giving touch propelled her ministry and her life. The result? A changed world.

Physical touch is mysterious. Parents recognize its power, but we forget about it. We coddle our toddlers, but as our kids grow, we release them from frequent touch. Usually, by the time they reach adolescence, we are uncomfortable with touching them altogether.

How do we touch them, when do we touch them, and where do we touch them? Teens recoil from touch—particularly in public, which affirms our discomfort with the whole thing. Thus, we feel hurt and confused, so we back off and abandon touch.

You can tell that teens like touch by looking around. Girls flirt with boys, provoking snowball fights or a hug. Teen boys, no less needy, invite touch through their demeanor and verbal communication. Ever see a football player give teammates a pat on the rear? Teens who receive healthy touch from peers receive acceptance and affirmation that they are worthy.

The touch of a parent reaches deeper. Teens who sense their identity and physique shifting need continual affirmation that they are valuable. Physical touch is a wonderful way to communicate this. Teens wonder if they should need their parents, sometimes hating the fact that they still do need their parents. Their bodies are changing, and their feelings are changing. Parental touch teaches them that they are loved amidst the multitude of changes.

I am privileged to care for teen girls in our local halfway home. These are girls who couldn't get along with parents or were freshly released from juvenile prisons. I have noticed among them high rates of sexual abuse, promiscuity, physical abuse, and physical fighting. They came to the home with a history of being touched in a vicious manner, and their behavior reflected this wrong touch. Those who were sexually assaulted perpetually sought out sex with others. Those who had been hit picked fights to hit back.

The manner in which teens have been touched changes their lives. Bad touch begets bad touch. Sexual assault begets promiscuity. Being slapped stimulates hitting, scratching, and physically pummeling others, but healthy touch teaches strength and dignity.

Inasmuch as these teens endured unhealthy touch, they lacked edifying touch. None reported being hugged or caressed by an important adult. Interestingly, they combed one another's hair and brought stuffed animals with them in order to have something to hug.

To those parents uncomfortable with touching teens, a few encouragements are in order: Do it and don't be afraid. Touch a teen's shoulders, hair, and head. At first a teen may recoil, leaving you feeling rejected and hurt. But remember this is a reflection of his discomfort with himself.

Gently persist but don't give up. Be respectful of the time and place. Touch him briefly but lovingly in private, not in public. What better way to teach sons manliness and security than by teaching them to receive love in the form of a hug? If they learn to receive touch and tenderness, they will be more secure in touching and giving love to others.

Fathers, hug your daughters and your sons. Adolescent girls learn to accept and like their physique when their father touches them appropriately. A father's touch to his daughter teaches her that her body is beautiful, dignified and worth preserving. His touch can affirm positive feelings about her sexuality, teaching her that her body is hers.

If Mother Teresa's touch was healing to strangers, imagine how much more restorative a parental touch will be to teens needing intimacy. If you are uncomfortable, keep trying. Their need is greater than our discomfort.

EMOTIONAL INTIMACY

Touch sets the tone in the relationship between parents and teens. Remember, intimacy occurs when one is open. Bringing emotional intimacy means creating and maintaining emotional connectedness with our teens. Many parents may believe the statement "being connected with teens" to be an oxymoron, but stay with me.

Emotional connectedness does not mean agreeing with or identifying with our teens. In fact, identifying with them too often as a buddy can breed insecurity because it breaks down necessary parental-teen intimacy.

Emotional intimacy occurs when parents invite a teen to divulge his insecurities, thoughts, and feelings. This means presenting numerous opportunities for this to occur and remaining calm when those thoughts spill forth.

First, recognize that teens decide to open up only when they feel they will be accepted. If parents are angry, cold, or aloof, teens will clam up. If parents are preoccupied, they will avoid us. If we are physically unavailable, they have no chance but to avail their feelings or thoughts to others. To further complicate matters, teens act impulsively and could open up at awkward moments.

But we needn't have a Ph.D. in communications to provide emotional intimacy for our teens. Let's review a few key communication skills to enhance intimacy with our teens.

1. When available, be available.

Nothing is more frustrating than talking to someone who isn't listening. We frustrate our teens by trying to listen while performing other tasks. If he wants to talk, sit down and look at him. Make eye contact, quiet your hands, and use body language that says, "I'm listening." Sitting and looking at him for a ten-minute conversation will make him feel that no one else exists in the world except for him. That's a great feeling.

2.   Listen first, speak last.

When a teen has something pressing on her heart and is willing to reveal it to you, fight the urge to jump in mid-sentence and rebut what she is saying. If you wait to respond until the end, she will listen more attentively because she believes that you are absorbing what she is saying. You may lose any two-way communication if you interrupt.

Honestly, listening to teens can be painful. First, we don't often agree. They may not make sense, and their fervor communicates more emotion than reason. When listening and speaking, fight the urge to be defensive. Your interrupting and repeating yourself only causes her to tune you out.

After you have listened and allowed her to express herself, speak firmly using fewer words. Parents often feel a need to justify their decisions and thoughts with flowing rebuttals. Remember, be assured that your authority as a parent gives her security, which is vital to her healthy development. You may want to explain why you are responding in a certain way to help her understand, but you don't need to justify every single point.

3.   Don't feel pressured to change him on the spot.

When a teen divulges his feelings, parents are often tempted to correct him. Usually we try arguing his point, and if that fails, we have ways of humiliating a child. Parents will gain greater influence by listening, waiting, and saying little in a quiet, unharried tone than by repeatedly arguing points raised by a teen.

Parents often feel panicked to resolve the issue quickly (during the argument at hand), and we worry that we will not have another opportunity to influence our teen regarding the issue. This is usually not true. Influence takes time. How much more effective we can be if we simply wait and listen, then conclude with the spoken resolve to think about their ideas for a while. When we regroup with our teens to reopen the issue, we will have their ear and respect because we didn't overreact or shoot them down.

4. Create time for intimacy to occur.

While intimacy cannot be contrived, time must be set aside in case it occurs. Teens see us prioritize our lives by watching how we spend our time and our money. If they see us working, watching TV, or exercising constantly and failing to allocate time for them, they infer (accurately) that they are not a priority. If a teen feels that he is not important, he will not divulge his "self" to a parent because it would be too risky.

Creating time simply means carving out one-on-one periods together. This can range from a car ride or dinner out together. The purpose of the time—once every week or two—is simply to communicate that you want to know how he is feeling about life, school, family, peers, etc.

You don't need to have an agenda or teach her "a lesson." You are simply availing your time and attention to her. If she fails to divulge herself, this is fine because there will be other times in the future.

Caution is warranted here. Parents whose schedules are full often feel pressured to "accomplish" something during special one-on-one times with teens. Please avoid this temptation. Sensing that we must achieve something sets both parent and teen up for frustration. Expectations should be minimal. It is simply a time to show that you enjoy being with her.

5. Enter into a situation where the two of you are mutually vulnerable.

Nothing binds two together like withstanding outside pressure alongside one another. Families who endure hardship either increase their strength by drawing together or fall apart.

The Hiding Place by Corrie ten Boom beautifully illustrates this. In this intriguing book, Corrie describes the experiences she had with her father and sister Betsie hiding Jews in the attic of their Dutch home during the Nazi occupation. They were caught by the Gestapo and sent to a prison camp.

As her biography unfolds, one can see the tenacious emotional bonds growing between Corrie, Betsie, and their father. Together they collaborated and risked their lives for their Jewish friends. Together they were discovered and dragged to prison camp. Together they endured harsh treatment, and when they were separated, their intimacy gave them strength to endure future hardships.

I think of Corrie's book when girls come into my office struggling with *anorexia* problems, which often stem from overdomination by a parent. One of my recommendations is to disrupt the family dynamic by asking them to take a "hard" vacation, such as camping in the wild. Camping thrusts family members into a position of mutual need and mutual vulnerability. Asking a parent to endure the elements with the anorexic daughter and other family members allows the parent to ask for help.

If they are successful in leaning upon one another, intimacy soars. Outside pressures have a way of illuminating the weaknesses and strength of individuals. When this occurs, family members draw closer—exchanging encouragement, help, and advice.

SPIRITUAL INTIMACY

Participants of Alcoholics Anonymous are endowed with a recognition that forces greater than themselves influence human behavior. Many acknowledge this force as being God, who is personal and real. Those who acknowledge God as this greater force converse with Him through prayer and allow themselves to spiritually connect. Prayer allows them an opportunity to open their hearts and minds to be seen by God. Prayer offers intimacy that cannot be received through human relationships precisely because mystery and divine interaction is involved.

Those in organizations like AA who acknowledge God as their higher power are not alone in their claims regarding healing and special connectedness with God. In fact, numerous medical reports have clearly documented the positive effect of religious participation on health. In an independent study, David Larson, M.D. and Susan Larson, M.A.T., discussed a large assortment of medical studies and concluded, "The comprehensive review of nearly 250 epidemiological studies found positive associations between religious commitment and health."[63]

Religious commitment includes prayer, affiliation with a church, and regular church attendance. Surveying the research prompted these authors to further state, "In general, these studies suggest that infrequent religious attendance should be regarded as a consistent risk factor for morbidity and mortality of various types."[64] Coming from the medical community, this is a very strong statement, suggesting that lack of spiritual connectedness is as serious as not taking life-saving medication.

The famous psychoanalyst Carl Jung felt the same way when he said in 1932, "Among all my patients in the second half of my life, there has not been one whose problem in the last resort was not that of finding a religious outlook on life. It is safe to say that every one of them fell ill because he had lost that which the living religions of every age have given their followers, and none of them has been really healed who did not regain his religious outlook."[65]

My own experience with patients supports these statements. Those who have convoluted relationships with parents, for example, find healing through connecting with a God who is perfect, safe, and powerful. Acknowledging the existence of God removes the possibility of complete aloneness—so often felt by teens struggling through their parents' divorce or rejection by their peers. God is all-present, all-loving, and all-embracing. He gives them entrance to the supernatural while at the same time offering a tangible moral plumb line.

In fact, studies further show that "religiosity" serves as a protective factor against high-risk behaviors for teens. These studies state that teens who profess a faith in God get into trouble less. Perhaps they strive to adhere to higher standards, but I suspect something deeper is involved—prayer. Prayer works for adults, and it works for teens.

Teens are less jaded than many adults, and their spirituality often feels more natural to them. For teens who are open to God, they should be allowed a relationship with Him.

Chapter Nineteen

MEETING THE LOVE NEEDS

Love is most nearly itself
When here and now cease to matter.
Old men ought to be explorers
Here and there does not matter
We must be still and still moving
Into another intensity.

T.S. ELIOT

WHEN IT COMES TO TEACHING TEENS TO GIVE AND RECEIVE love, teaching via the spoken word proves woefully inadequate. The need to be loved and to extend love is fundamental to survival of the human heart. Since the family unit is the first source of love for kids, it is the primary place in which they learn to give and receive love.

If the love exchange fails in this primary arena, reteaching it can be almost impossible. Thus, parents have a serious burden. We must love well if our teens are to love well. This sounds simple until we come to grips with the fact that we parents can be poor models of love. Intellectually, loving children unconditionally sounds easy, but in reality it is very difficult. Why is this?

First, loving teens is frightening. Someone once remarked that loving children is like carrying our hearts outside of our bodies. Loving our teens feels frightening because we don't want it taken away or crushed. The more deeply we love, the more vulnerable we feel. Strong parents must be vulnerable to heartache but also willing to endure heartache if it leads to loving our teens.

Sometimes loving our teens feels more frightening than it need be. Parents who perceive that they need something from their teens set themselves up for tremendous hurt. Those who look to teens to fill their own needs for companionship, value, or intimacy—to name a few—will experience deep hurt when the teen fails to "give" what the parent expects.

Conversely, if a parent who looks for these things from the teen "finds" them in the relationship, love again disappoints because an unhealthy dimension has been added to the love. In fact, parents don't need companionship from teens. We may want it, but we don't need it. Needing such muddies the love relationship and makes it more frightening because we feel more vulnerable. The problem isn't with parents' ability regarding love, but with their perception regarding their needs in the relationship with their teens.

When parents need little from teens, they are more free to love. Expectation goes down and love becomes more pure and unconditional. Is it appropriate to desire certain things from teens? Certainly. But desire is not need. Desire stems from a heart that is fundamentally satisfied while need erupts from one that has been shattered and looks toward the teen in order to have the brokenness repaired. The scary thing is that often this dynamic occurs subconsciously.

Second, love is uncomfortable. Let's face it, there are times in most parents' lives when we have difficulty expressing love to our teens. Tension rises over rules, behavior, and schoolwork, which leaves us angry and frustrated. Loving is hard when we are disappointed and angry. Teens recognize this and even play on it in order to manipulate and frustrate parents further.

So what should parents do? We need to love them anyway—a tough but not impossible assignment. Loving teens well does not mean feeling nice about them or agreeing with them. It means recognizing that we are the adults and they are the children. Love is not simply a feeling, it is a decision.

Loving teens can be quite gritty. Parents must resolve to love because sometimes if resolve is not severe, love—or at least the expression of love—fails.

Love is uncomfortable because it commands that we communicate with teens even when the relationship is rocky. Love encompasses a desire to endure hardships and heartaches with teens. Love believes in their ability to excel in a far greater degree than they ever imagined. Love communicates hope around each impending corner.

Third, love is richer when we have nothing to lose by loving. Loving teens is personal, which is why parents of teens are often afraid to express love for fear they will look foolish or their teens will reject them. In reality, if parental love is genuine what child can refuse it?

We parents don't want to feel rejected so sometimes we distance ourselves from our teens in order to avoid rejection. We are afraid we will lose something if we love and our teens don't love back. What will we lose? Our self-esteem, our sense of being a good parent—maybe even our happiness. The truth is if we don't look to our teens to provide these things in the first place, we really won't lose any of them. Healthy parenting means finding self-esteem, companionship, and happiness apart from our teens. These must come from our spouse or from God.

Sandy was a seventeen-year-old boy struggling with depression. His parents were married, and he was an excellent student. The root of his depression lay in his perception that his dad didn't love him, but his father insisted that this wasn't so.

As I asked questions, I learned that their history of their communication revealed that Sandy's father never expressed love in a positive way. He continually criticized Sandy verbally, and his body language repeatedly communicated disapproval. When asked if this was true, Sandy's father said yes, and he divulged that while he loved Sandy and wanted to break the cycle of criticism, he also was deeply afraid of expressing love for fear of being rejected or looking "stupid."

Sandy's father needn't harbor those fears. He had nothing to lose by loving well.

TEACHING TEENS TO GIVE LOVE

Clearly we have a responsibility in modeling healthy love to our teens if we want them to mature into loving, strong adults. One way we can do that is by teaching them to serve others. Teens who are given the opportunity to look beyond themselves and their interests find tremendous joy in serving those outside of their own small sphere.

Community service and local mission work teaches teens to be "other-centered," visibly illustrating that what they have to offer is important in the lives of others. Volunteer work builds their self-esteem and teaches them about their own wonderful ability to love. Many parents caught in the frenzy of overpacked schedules simply forget about teaching teens to serve, but service is an important learning ground for teens.

TEACHING TEENS TO RECEIVE LOVE

Since all of us are wired to receive love, failing to do so happens only when there is a lack of trust, anger, sadness, and depression.

Teens who have been hurt repeatedly close themselves to receiving love. Teens who perceive continual criticism from parents refuse their love. Parents who respond to confrontation by withdrawing and refusing to talk are not giving teens a chance to receive love.

Four basic parenting styles contribute to interrupting the love exchange:

1. The domineering parents are quick to end conflict by assuming an authoritative posture. These parents leave teens wanting for love, usually because they never felt worthy of their parents' love.

2. The "anything goes" parents are insecure in their authority as a parent so they release it altogether. These parents make the teen uncomfortable because there are no boundaries, and the focus of the relationship is friendship rather than parenting. Teens wonder if parental love is trustworthy.

3. The detached parents are afraid of closeness with their teens. These parents generally recognize this and extend invitations to love erratically and unpredictably. Divorced parents often wind up here. They have experienced such pain from the marital breakup that they withdraw altogether from their parenting duties.

4. The passive parents feel impotent to assert themselves or "take" what the world dishes out. These parents realize that something is wrong in their parenting, so they compensate by indulging teens and abandoning healthy rules. Teens can become quite manipulative with passive parents, playing on their guilt to get whatever they want.

Some parents tend to fit into only one of these four styles, while others fall into different categories during difficult stages of their lives. My purpose is to teach us to recognize our own downfalls as parents in order to restore healthy relationships with our kids. Teens need our love, and most teens love us in spite of our parenting quirks.

I encourage you, with the help of a supportive spouse or adult friend, to have the courage to examine your style of communication with your teen. Then try to view the way you communicate through the eyes of your teens. What are they seeing? Are they correct in perceiving continual criticism, lack of guidance, or an overly needy love from you?

MEETING THE NEED TO HAVE VALUE

Lovability and capability: the two should never meet. Teens who have embraced their lovability are emotionally sound individuals with a positive sense of self-worth. These teens draw on this knowledge to experiment with their capability. They are able to do so because they feel they can fail yet still be loved for who they are. If they succeed, they feel great, but their success pales in comparison to the experience of being loved.

Where do problems lie? First, in our zeal to help teens improve self-esteem, we fall prey to linking lovability with capability. Encouraging teens to use their natural talents is easy. We look around, find a sports team, buy a musical instrument, and sign them up. We may utter a few encouraging words to bolster them. They begin to succeed and we feel great.

Why? Because if they are successful, we are successful, but sometimes when they become very successful, they have to continue to succeed to make us feel good. This temptation must be guarded against.

TEACHING CAPABILITY

Success in various arenas serves two purposes: to illuminate natural gifts and to identify and encourage capability. Teens who are sensitive and compassionate should be applauded, and these emotional gifts should be verbally recognized by parents. If their intellects are unusual, they should be supported to broaden their thinking and the subjects they take. If teens are physically adept, placing them into competitive leagues helps them realize their capacity to excel.

Since gifts vary among teens, parents must do detective work to recognize them. There are universal lessons that are important for the development of healthy self-esteem in all teens. They are the following:

1. Teaching teens self-control.

I am a strong proponent of sexual abstinence during the teen years because I believe it would be malpractice to teach otherwise when you consider disease risk and psychological trauma. I also believe sexual control to be a prime avenue through which teens learn self-control. Exerting control in an otherwise out-of-control culture will send their self-esteem soaring. Medically, teens deserve to be disease-free.

Parents, physicians, educators, and society recognize alcohol, drugs, cigarettes, and violence as high-risk behaviors for teens. Please be aware that medical literature always includes sexual activity in the above list, yet our approach toward dealing with teen sexual activity is markedly different than our approach to the other four.

Tobacco companies, albeit reluctantly, are campaigning to decrease teen smoking, as witnessed by the death of Joe Camel. The government institutes laws forbidding teen drinking, and there are publicly funded programs to help teens stay away from drugs. In these areas we do not compromise our message to youth, which is: Don't take drugs, don't drink, don't smoke, and don't solve your problems through violence. The expectation is also clear: we expect that you (teens) can control your behavior, and we adults will do everything we can to help you do so.

Then we come to sex. Yes, it most certainly is a high-risk behavior, though I'm convinced many don't believe so. The prevailing attitude is that sex is fun, harmless, and besides, teens really can't control themselves anyway. On some intellectual level, our lack of conviction gives free license to teen sex.

Let's look at what we teach our teens about sexual behavior. We give them plumbing lessons, and then ask them to make sure they use protection. Teaching teens that engaging in sexual activity with "protection" (for the body, of course, not for the heart) is like teaching kids that it's okay to smoke as long as they use filtered cigarettes. We would never do this, and we must do exactly the same regarding sexual activity. Sex is not for unmarried kids.

Can teens refrain from sexual activity? You may not think so, but studies show that roughly one-half of the teen population is not sexually active. We can teach teens to control their intense sexual feelings by reminding them that they have a choice regarding their actions and that their feelings don't have to dictate the decisions they make. Teens learning these two very important skills will have a tremendously enhanced sense of self-control.

2.   Teaching teens to separate emotions from behavior.

Some may disagree, but a glance at the evening news reveals a culture driven by their emotions. Miserable feelings cause adults to drink and drive, and fatal car accidents occur. We have seen way too many emotional teens and even preteens bring guns to school and kill schoolmates. We are a culture that has given free reign to emotions and destructive behavior.

Teen girls who starve themselves experience anger and depression that goes often unrecognized. Internalized anger and sadness feel out of control, and girls act on those feelings either by starving or vomiting. Therapeutic interventions strive to separate feelings from behavior, teaching girls that they don't have to act on those feelings by starving or vomiting.

Teen boys who can embrace their emotions and urges regarding sexual activity but refrain from acting upon them find their self-esteem heightened because separating their feelings from their actions bolster the significance of each.

Teaching this separation is at the foundation of healthy maturity. Remember the sense of lost control? This exercise restores that control and when it is successful, the benefits far surpass the losses. Teens need to know that they are capable of intense feelings and then choosing how they will act with respect to those feelings. Our culture lures them to believe they have no choice. But they do have a choice, which can allow their sense of value to soar.

The best way to teach teens is to begin asking them questions about how they feel. Parents must be persistent because often teens don't want to talk. But if parents are gentle and sincere, teens will eventually open up on a variety of issues. If they are uncomfortable talking about deeply personal feelings, start with some safe issues like how they feel about a new teacher, a new kid on the block, or their favorite celebrity or sports star. Then move on to more significant feelings such as peer pressure, the opposite sex, and their future.

3. Teaching teens that emotions don't need to control behavior.

My personal belief after reviewing the literature on adolescent depression and the incidence of high-risk behaviors is that we have never experienced such confusion, loneliness, and aberrant behaviors in teens as we experience today.

These teens don't know what they feel. Some have felt so much pain that they have dived into numbness. Some have lost so much hope that they are showing the world how ugly they really feel. We adults must do more than help them sort out their emotions. We can agree that their feelings are powerful and explosive at times—but they are just feelings. Once teens practice this, they feel incredibly good about themselves.

Sexual restraint is another action that allows them to exercise this truth. High school-age teens keenly know how strong sexual feelings can be, but if they are taught that these feelings are healthy and normal-and still controllable-they will be much better off in the long run. That's what we want for our teens, isn't it?

Chapter Twenty

WAGING WAR

No one conquers who doesn't fight.

GABRIEL BIEL

WHILE MOST ADULTS INTELLECTUALLY AGREE THAT OUR value is not determined by appearance or how others see us, our lives reveal the opposite. We spend billions of dollars on cosmetics, diet plans, exercise equipment, and fashion magazines to improve the way we look. This is fine if we're pursuing better health to improve quality of life and reduce disease risk.

But notice how emaciated models are forced to be. The fashion industry sends a loud message to our young women—thin is good and thinner is better. And the waif message extends to a deeper level: become weak, not strong. Evaporate and don't lend an assertive posture emotionally, physically, or intellectually.

Don't remark on a teen girl's figure if you don't want your comment to be significant. If a teen boy is lifting weights and you don't want his muscle size to define him, don't say anything about it.

Parents, relatives, and family friends often feel complimentary when they remark on a teen's recent weight loss, enhanced beauty, or larger muscles. *Don't do it!* Resist the urge to make comments such as, "Oh, you look so good. Have you lost weight?"

Don't joke about a boy's ability to "get" any girl he pleases. Such comments seem benign, but they perpetuate a notion that how a teen looks is linked to his or her value. Can you ask about their intellectual accomplishments or physical challenges rather than commenting on their looks? This is a small but important beginning in dethroning weight and vanity from their positions of importance.

ATHLETIC INVOLVEMENT

Whenever teens participate in athletic events, particularly competitive ones, serious caution must be taken by parents. In our zeal, we parents can tip teens into a dangerous territory regarding self-esteem as it relates to their athletic capability.

Entire families disrupt schedules for teen (and preteen) athletic events. Thousands of dollars can be poured into their athletic pursuits, enlarging the significance of them in their lives. This not only places pressure on them to succeed, but it also gives teens two false messages.

The first is that athletic success and intensity are more important than participation and enjoyment. The second is that teens learn a frightening and destabilizing sense of power when so much emphasis is focused upon their athletic pursuits. They see that their participation is the center of the family's priorities and even family finances. They see their parents running them to and from practice and sports events, which leads them to believe they are the central figures in the home.

Perspective is needed here. Athletics are a wonderful medium through which teens can recognize their capabilities. If we allow them to let their sport define who they are, however, what happens to their sense of identities if and when they lose? But if sports participation augments their characters, they draw strength from their previous accomplishments and move forward.

Is your sports involvement out of balance? Why is Tom playing hockey six nights a week and on Sunday afternoons? Does he want to be an Olympian? Unless your child is a prodigy and playing at an elite level, such a rigorous schedule may not be warranted and furthermore may be even harmful.

If you want Sarah to tap dance for fun, fight for her right to do so. If you want Will to be a well-rounded athlete, take him out of summer hockey and let him play soccer. Parents succumbing to pressure from coaches to play one sport year-round set up the child for burnout.

I realize that many teens are working toward college scholarships. These kids need intense athletic focus for a time. But many teens are not collegiate caliber, so why burn them out long before their junior or senior years? If your child is an exceptional athlete, the onus is on your shoulders to be certain that she knows that her value is not derived from her athletic accomplishments.

You have a greater responsibility because she must know that she is lovable whether she continues to excel or leaves athletics behind. Tell her how much she means to you and that athletics tale second place. You may have to assume, however, that she believes athletic accomplishments define her, which means that you should gear your speech and actions toward reversing that thinking.

Physically, their young bodies may not be able to handle intense athletic demands, which I classify as four or more practices per week. But the physical ramifications of athletic overinvolvement are just the tip of the iceberg. Teens can mentally burn out, which leads them to feel like a failure.

Healthy parenting means determining what you and your teens want out of their athletic experiences. Then resolve to provide this for them.

VERBALIZE POSITIVE FEELINGS

Any good marriage book reminds spouses to frequently communicate positive feelings about each other. Since women are more relationship-driven, they need to talk more about their feelings. Both husband and wife, however, need frequent words of affirmation to enhance their positive feelings about themselves and their marital relationship.

If mature adults need words of encouragement, think how much more teens need them. During a phase of life that feels so confusing, teens can't afford to be left wondering how their significant loved ones feel about them. They need to be told repeatedly that you love them—something that parents can't tell their teens too often.

I encourage parents to make at least one statement of affirmation daily to their teen. These statements should not refer to physical or intellectual accomplishments, but something along the lines of "I love you" or "You're great" or "You are so special."

Often teens respond to parents' comments with a sour face or a "Yeah, right." Doesn't matter. Keep on saying them. Sometimes parents contend that words are not necessary since their child already "knows they are loved." No, they don't. Parents may know, but teens need to be reminded as they deal with the barrage of negative messages coming at them.

PROVIDING SAFETY

First-born teens have a tough row to hoe. They become a teenager first in the family, and the excitement of entering the teen years is particularly keen for parents. Mom and Dad see that she is growing up, and as is the case with most first-borns, they expect her to act grown up. By the time the second-born enters the teen years, however, parents have learned some painful lessons about how immature teens can be.

The rules begin to tighten. Why? Because teens can behave like toddlers in adult bodies. They have temper tantrums and do absolute-ly foolish things. My neighbor recently reprimanded her teenage son after she discovered him making a movie in their back yard. I know Matthew. He's a great kid, responsible and bright. During one scene in his movie project, he removed his shirt, donned a cape and ran twenty-five yards across his backyard (where the snow was beginning to melt) with his mom's sharpest butcher knife in his hand. He could have slipped on the ice and done who knows what.

Was he crazy? No! He was a teen who lacked mature thinking. What does he need? Physical boundaries and sensible rules to keep him safe.

The peak times for accidental death of kids are during the toddler years and the teen years. In the latter time period, the toys are more dangerous. Rules must be made regarding cars, alcohol, dating, and anything else that is life-threatening. Teens hate rules, but boundaries must be made and serious consequences must follow if rules are broken.

I encourage parents to create a list of a few "non-negotiable" areas where parents insist on being in charge. If the rule falls outside of the "non-negotiable" category, then parents can relax a bit more and allow the teens to help decide what they can or can't do.

PROVIDING PHYSICAL SAFETY

Studies reveal the key times that teens get into trouble are after school and evenings. When kids come home to an empty house, they do not have supervision and adult accountability. That means you need to get home as soon as possible.

With frightening regularity, the following scenario is reported to me by parents of my patients. It goes something like this:

Mom and Dad need to leave town for a weekend getaway or to take another child to an out-of-town event. Their teen son wants to stay home, so the parents let him. On past occasions, he has proven to be responsible, but this time around, the weekend turns out to be disastrous when he hosts a party and the house gets trashed. What the parents failed to factor in was not the responsible nature of their teen, but the immaturity of his peers, who messed up a home without an adult present.

I have literally seen thousands of dollars of damage done to homes by teens, but in fact, leaving a teen home alone was unfair to him. He was put in a situation over his head, and parents need to anticipate those vulnerable situations. Parents must guard teens from too much, too soon.

Teens quickly become immersed in their own peer culture at the onset of junior high or high school, and this is to be expected. Parents commonly make the mistake of abandoning their teens to this new subculture, relying on them to maneuver their way through peer groups, pick his own friends, attend after-school activities, and go to parties, etc.

I can't emphasize strongly enough how important it is for parents to know what their kids are up to. After letting them know that you are giving them freedom to make some decisions on their own, make them accountable for the time they spend away from you. Ask them to report to you regarding how they are spending their time.

If they want to go to a party, insist on knowing who will be there, including the adults. Remind your youngsters that if they ever find themselves in a situation where they are over their heads, they should call for help. They can phone you or another adult on a list they carry in their wallet-people such as youth pastors, school counselors, neighbors, or relatives.

A word about dating. Repeatedly, young girls enter into dating relationships that can be emotionally and physically risky. Since girls mature more quickly than boys during the early high school years, some begin romantic relationships with a boy several years older. In truth, this is not a fair situation for most girls. While they may feel they relate better to older boys, they are out of their league. They can be overpowered intellectually *and* physically.

Since they are not on equal ground, parents should keep girls from being placed in compromising situations. My belief is that ninth grade girls should date ninth grade boys, sophomores should date sophomores, juniors should date juniors, and seniors should date seniors.

This reminds me of the old fable about a father nurturing his son into manhood. Upon the thirteenth birthday of his son, the warrior took him deep into the woods for his initiation into adulthood. The father helped him carry supplies and make his own camp before leaving his son for the night. Upon arriving home the following day, his mother asked him, "How did your night go? Did any animals threaten you?"

"Not at all," the boy replied. "As a matter of fact, I never slept better in my life." Entering manhood, he concluded, was a piece of cake.

Somewhat confused, the mother went to her husband and told him about their conversation.

"This is what happened," he said. "Unbeknownst to our son, I stood watch behind a nearby tree throughout the night, and it's lucky I did. I speared two mountain lions prowling near his camp."

How cruel this father would have been to leave the boy out in the woods unprotected. In the same manner, we parents assume our teens are just as capable of withstanding sexual pressure, saying no to drugs and alcohol, and driving under the speed limit. Yet they are not adults, and they need us to stay nearby—behind the tree—for several more years.

PROVIDING EMOTIONAL SAFETY

If we agree that the feelings of teens are important, how can parents provide emotional safety?

Again, safety implies a comfortable, receptive environment wherein teens can express their emotions, determine (with adult guidance) their appropriateness, all within the context of a family safety net.

Parents often find this concept of providing an emotionally safe environment confusing and uncomfortable. First, we sense a teen's emotions erupting out of control, and we often can't fathom where the feelings come from. In truth, many teens don't know where their feelings come from. We don't always need to know, but if repeated patterns of disturbing eruptions occur, such as anger, then professional help should be sought.

Inviting Teens to Feel

Teens will usually express anger whether or not they feel safe in doing so. For many, temper tantrums become a way of life; they feel good. But many adolescents (particularly girls) may refrain from expressing anger—or any other emotion for that matter—if they anticipate being humiliated. Some parents will deflect a teen's anger by becoming angrier, and nobody wins under that scenario.

The best way to avoid anger situations is to have a house in which teens can share their feelings. For instance, if a boy divulges to his father that he was ridiculed in the locker room about his chest size and the father says, "Get on with it, guys will be guys," chances are he will refrain from expressing his hurt later on.

If this pattern continues, he eventually finds himself unable to accurately size up situations. He second-guesses his feelings, his thoughts, and his behavior. Finally, since his feelings are not acknowledged, he feels out of control, and when that happens, he can explode.

Emotional safety is not only an environment in which teens can express emotions, it is one in which teens receive teaching from parents about their emotions. If a father responds with compassion, looks his son in the eye, and says, "Tom, that must have really hurt your feelings. How did you feel when they said that?" his son will know it's safe to respond.

Teens whose feelings are never acknowledged are left guessing about their significance. Their feelings are never measured against another's, never discussed, never validated, or never weighed. The result is inordinately skewed perceptions of themselves and the world around them.

ERECTING BOUNDARIES

Specifically, I tell teens the following: "You can feel and express whatever you like, but here are the rules. You may not swear, raise your voice, or say anything berating me or yourself." They have room to roam within solid fences. Teens are not capable of being in charge of their emotions because they are not adults yet.

There has never been a time in history when teens needed adults more than they do right now. They need our teaching, our direction, and our unconditional love. If we sincerely endeavor to give these things to our teens, we will be well on our way to restoring their tender souls, and helping them bridge that chasm from teenagehood to adulthood.

ENDNOTES

1 Nouwen, Henri J.M. *The Genessee Diary: Report from a Trappist Monastery*. (Garden City, NY: Doubleday & Company, Inc., 1976).

2. Ibid.

3. David Allen, M.D. *Shattering the Gods Within* (Chicago: Moody Press, 1994) p. 30.

4. Ibid.

5. Ibid.

6. Brown, J.D., Childers, K.W., Waszak, C.S. "Television and Adolescent Sexuality," *Journal of Adolescent Health Care*, 1990; 11:62-70.

7. Daniel John Derksen, M.D. and Victor C. Strasburger M.D. "Children and the Influence of the Media," *Primary Care*, vol. 21 Number 4, December 1994.

8. Victor L. Strasburger, M.D. "Children, Adolescents, and Television," *Pediatrics Review*, Vol. 13, No. 4, April 1992, p. 144.

9. Ibid.

10. Jeremiah S. Strouse, Nancy Buerkel-Rothfuss, and Edgar L.J. Long, "Gender and Family As Moderators of the Relationship Between Music Video Exposure and Adolescent Sexual Permissiveness," *Adolescence*, vol. 30, No. 119, Fall 1995, p. 505.

11. Ibid.

12. Victor L. Strasburger, M.D., "Children, Adolescents, and Television," *Pediatrics Review*, Vol. 13, No. 4, April 1992, p. 144.

13. Hayes, C.D., editor, *Risking the Future: Adolescent Sexuality, Pregnancy, and Childbearing*, (Washington, D.C.: National Academy Press, 1987) vol. 1.

14. Kirby, Ph.D., et al. "School-Based Programs to Reduce Sexual Risk Behaviors: A Review of Effectiveness," *Public Health Reports*, May-June 1994, Vol. 109, No. 3, p. 339.

15. Ibid, p. 339.

16. Victor L. Strasburger, M.D., "Children, Adolescents, and Television," *Pediatrics Review,* Vol. 13, No. 4, April 1992, p. 144.

17. Denise B. Kandel, Ph.D. and Mark Davies, M.P.H., "High School Students Who Use Crack and Other Drugs," *Archives of General Psychiatry,* Vol. 53, January 1996.

18. Johnston, L.D., O'Malley, P.M. & Bachman, J.G. (19936), National Survey Results on Drug Use From the Monitoring The Future Study, 1975-1992 (Rockville, MD: National Institute on Drug Abuse).

19. Phyllis L. Ellickson, et al, "Teenagers and Alcohol Misuse in the United States: by any definition, It's a Big Problem," *Addiction,* 1996, 91 (10), p. 1489.

20.Parmelee, Dean X., *Child and Adolescent Psychiatry* (St. Louis, MO: 1996), p. 240.

21. Ibid.

22. Michael Resnick, Ph.D. et al, "Protecting Adolescents From Harm," *Journal of the American Medical Association,* 10 September 1997, Vol. 278, No. 10.

23. Ibid.

24. "Safe Sex" (An unpublished manual with a collection of medical research papers), Medical Institute for Sexual Health slide program, lecture notes, and supplemental materials. Version 3.0, (Austin, Texas: 1995) p. 5.

25. Ibid. p. 2.

26. Apuzzle, J.J. and Pelosi, M.A., "The New Salpingitis Subtle Symptoms, Aggressive Management," *The Female Patient,* 14 Nov. 1989.

27. "Safe Sex" (An unpublished manual with a collection of medical research papers), Medical Institute for Sexual Health slide program, lecture notes, and supplemental materials. Version 3.0, (Austin, Texas: 1995) p. 5.

28. Gonik, B., "Pelvic Inflammation Disease in the Adolescent," *Texas Medicine,* 83 February 1987.

29. "Safe Sex" (An unpublished manual with a collection of medical research papers), Medical Institute for Sexual Health slide program, lecture notes, and supplemental materials. Version 3.0, (Austin, Texas: 1995).

30. "Sexual Health Today," Medical Institute of Austin, Texas, p. 76. (This is a collection of articles.)

31. Ibid.

32. Ibid.

33. "Safe Sex" (An unpublished manual with a collection of medical research papers), Medical Institute for Sexual Health slide program, lecture notes, and supplemental materials. Version 3.0, (Austin, Texas: 1995) p. 5.

34. Ibid.

35. Ibid.

36. "Safe Sex" (An unpublished manual with a collection of medical research papers), Medical Institute for Sexual Health slide program, lecture notes, and supplemental materials. Version 3.0, (Austin, Texas: 1995).

37. Ibid.

38. "Sexual Health Today," Medical Institute of Austin, Texas, p. 76. (This is a collection of articles.)

39. Ibid.

40. "Safe Sex" (An unpublished manual with a collection of medical research papers), Medical Institute for Sexual Health slide program, lecture notes, and supplemental materials. Version 3.0, (Austin, Texas: 1995).

41. Ibid.

42. "Safe Sex" (An unpublished manual with a collection of medical research papers), Medical Institute for Sexual Health slide program, lecture notes, and supplemental materials. Version 3.0, (Austin, Texas: 1995) p. 5.

43. "Sexual Health Today," Medical Institute of Austin, Texas, p. 76. (This is a collection of articles.)

44. Ibid.

45. Ibid.

46. Institute of Medicine, *The Hidden Epidemic–Confronting Sexually Transmitted Disease*, edited by Thomas R. Eng and William T. Butler, (Washington D.C.: National Academy Press, 1997), p. 33.

47. Cappelli, et al., "Identifying Depression and Suicidal Adolescents in a Teen Health Clinic," *Journal of Adolescent Health*, 1995, 16:64-70.

48. *Morbidity and Mortality Weekly Report*, September 1996, vol. 45/No.ss-4.

49. Besseghini, Victoria. "Depression and Suicide in Children and Adolescents," *Annals New York Academy of Sciences*, 1995, pgs. 94-97.

50. Frank B. Minirth, M.D. and Paul D. Meier, *Happiness is a Choice,* (Baker Book House Company: 1978), p. 108.

51. Ibid.

52. Parmelee, Dean X., *Child and Adolescent Psychiatry* (St. Louis, MO: 1996), p. 123-126.

53. Peter M. Lewinsoh, Paul Rohde, and John R. Seeley, "Psychosocial Risk Factors for Future Adolescent Suicide Attempts," *Journal of Consulting and Clinical Psychology,* 1994, Vol. 62, No. 2, pp. 297-305.

54. Ibid.

55. "Sexual Health Today," Medical Institute of Austin, Texas, p. 76. (This is a collection of articles.)

56. Independent Evaluation Study, Best Friends Foundation, 1995, Washington, D.C.

57. Melvin L. Silberman, *The Experience of Schooling* (New York: Holt, Rinehart & Winston, Inc., 1971), p. 108-111.

58. Ibid.

59. Ibid.

60. Michael Resnick, Ph.D. et al, "Protecting Adolescents From Harm," *Journal of the American Medical Association,* 10 September 1997, Vol. 278, No. 10.

61. Ibid.

62. Ibid.

63. David B. Larson, M.D., M.S.P.H. and Susan S. Larson, M.A.T., "The Forgotten Factor In Physical and Mental Health: What Does the Research Show?" An independent study seminar, 1994, p. 120.

64. Ibid.

65. Ibid.

BIBLIOGRAPHY

Barnes, Grace M., et al. "Changes in Alcohol Use and Alcohol-Related Problems among 7th to 12th Grade Students in New York State, 1983-1994." *Alcoholism: Clinical and Experimental Research*, 1997.

Bates, Marsha E. and Labouvie, Erich W. "Adolescent Risk Factors and the Prediction of Persistent Alcohol and Drug Use into Adulthood." *Alcoholism: Clinical and Experimental Research*, vol. 21, 1997.

Besseghini, Victoria H. "Depression and Suicide in Children and Adolescents." *Annals New York Academy of Sciences*, 1995.

Cappelli, Mario, Ph.D., et al. "Identifying Depressed and Suicidal Adolescents in a Teen Health Clinic." *Journal of Adolescent Health*, 1995.

Coker, Ann L., et al. "Correlates and Consequences of Early Initiation of Sexual Intercourse." *Journal of School Health*, November 1994.

Daves, Jennifer A., M.A. "Addressing Television Sexuality With Adolescents." *Pediatric Annals*, February 1995.

Derksen, Daniel John, M.D. and Strasburger, Victor C., M.D. "Children and the Influence of the Media." *Primary Care*, December 1994.

Elkind, David. *The Hurried Child*. Massachusetts: Addison-Wesley Publishing Company, 1981.

Ellickson, Phyllis L, et al. "Teenagers and Alcohol Misuse in the United States: by Any Definition It's a Big Problem." *Addiction*, 1996.

Fahey, Patrick J., M.D., et al. "Primary Care: Clinics in Office Practice." *Adolescent Medicine*, March 1998.

Fergusson, David M., et al. "Alcohol Misuse and Juvenile Offending in Adolescence." *Addiction*, 1996.

Fisher, Terri D. "Family Communication and the Sexual Behavior and Attitudes of College Students." *Journal of Youth and Adolescence*, vol. 16, 1987.

Graber, Julia A., Ph.D. and Brooks-Gunn, Jeanne, Ph.D. "Models of Development: Understanding Risk in Adolescence." *Suicide and Life-Threatening Behavior*, 1995.

Hays, Ron D. and Ellickson, Phyllis L. "What is Adolescent Alcohol Misuse in the United States According to the Experts?" *Alcohol & Alcoholism*, vol 31, 1996.

Howard, Marion and McCabe, Judith B. "Helping Teenagers Postpone Sexual Involvement." *Family Planning Perspectives*, February 1990.

Jones-Webb, Rhonda, Dr. P.H., et al. "Relationships Among Alcohol Availabilty, Drinking Location, Alcohol Consumption, and Drinking Problems in Adolescents." *Substance Use and Misuse*, 1997.

Kandel, Denise B., Ph.D. and Davies, Mark, M.P.H. "High School Students Who Use Crack and Other Drugs." *Arch Gen Psychiatry*, January 1996.

Kingsley, Lawrence A., Dr.PH., et al. "Sexual Transmission Efficiency of Hepatitis B Virus and Human Immunodeficiency Virus Among Heterosexual Men." *Journal of the American Medical Association*, July 11, 1990.

Kirby, Douglas, Ph.D. et al. "School-Based Programs to Reduce Sexual Risk Behaviors: A Review of Effectiveness." *Public Health Reports*, May-June 1994.

Klein, Jonathan D., et al. "Adolescents' Risky Behavior and Mass Media Use." *Pediatrics*, July 1993.

Koopman, Cheryl, Ph.D., et al. "Assessment of Knowledge of AIDS and Beliefs About AIDS Prevention Among Adolescents." *AIDS Education and Prevention*, 1990.

Krowchuk, Daniel P., M.D. "Sexually Transmitted Diseases in Adolescents: What's New? *Southern Medical Journal*, February 1998.

Ku, Leighton, Ph.D., M.P.H., et al. "Factors Influencing First Intercourse for Teenage Men." *Public Health Reports*, November-December 1993.

Lempers, Jacques D. and Clark-Lempers, Dania S. "Economic Hardship, Family Relationships, And Adolescent Distress: An Evaluation of a Stress-Distress Mediation Model in Mother-Daughter and Mother-Son Dyads." *Adolescence*, Summer 1997.

Lewinsohn, Peter M.; Rohde, Paul; and Seeley, John R. "Alcohol Consumption in High School Adolescents: Frequency of Use and Dimensional Structure of Associated Problems." *Addiction*, 1996.

Lewinsohn, Peter M.; Rohde, Paul; and Seeley, John R. "Psychosocial Risk Factors for Future Adolescent Suicide Attempts." *Journal of Consulting and Clinical Psychology*, 1994, vol. 62.

Luster, Tom and Small, Stephen A. "Adolescent Sexual Activity: An Ecological, Risk-Factor Approach." *Journal of Marriage and the Family*, February 1994.

Luster, Tom and Small, Stephen A. "Factors Associated with Sexual Risk-Taking Behaviors Among Adolescents." *Journal of Marriage and the Family*, August 1994.

Massachusetts Medical Society. "Update: Trends in AIDS Incidence, Deaths, and Prevalence—United States, 1996." *Morbidity and Mortality Weekly Report*, February 28, 1997.

Morgan, Irene S. "Recognizing Depression in the Adolescent." *MCN*, June 1994.

Oh, M. Kim, M.D., et al. "Risk for Gonoccal and Chlamydial Cervicitis in Adolescent Females: Incidence and Recurrence in a Prospective Cohort Study." *Journal of Adolescent Health*, vol. 18, 1996.

Orr, Donald P., M.D., et al. "Premature Sexual Activity as an Indicator of Psychosocial Risk." *Pediatrics*, February 1991.

Patten, Christi A., et al. "Depressive Symptoms in California Adolescents: Family Structure and Parental Support." *Journal of Adolescent Health*, 1997; 20.

Resnick, Michael D., et al. "Protecting Adolescents From Harm: Findings from the National Longitudinal Study on Adolescent Health." *Journal of the American Medical Association*, September 10, 1997.

Rohde, Paul, et al. "Psychiatric Comorbidity with Problematic Alcohol Use in High School Students." *J. Am. Acad. Child Adolesc. Psychiatry*, January 1996.

Santelli, John S. and Beilenson, Peter. "Risk Factors for Adolescent Sexual Behavior, Fertility, and Sexually Transmitted Diseases." *Journal of School Health*, September 1992.

"Sexuality, Contraception, and the Media." *Pediatrics*, February 1995.

Sieving, Renee, Ph.D., et al. "Cognitive and Behavioral Predictors of Sexually Transmitted Disease Risk Behavior Among Sexually Active Adolescents." *Arch Pediatr Adolesc Med*, March 1997.

Stark, Kevin D. et al. "Cognitive Triad: Relationship to Depressive Symptoms, Parents' Cognitive Triad, and Perceived Parental Messages." *Journal of Abnormal Child Psychology*, vol. 24, 1996.

Strasburger, Victor C., M.D. "Adolescent Sexuality and the Media." *Pediatric Clinics of North America*, June 1989.

Strasburger, Victor C., M.D. "Children, Adolescents, and Television." *Pediatrics in Review*, April 1992.

Strouse, Jeremiah S., et al. "Gender and Family as Moderators of the Relationship Between Music Video Exposure and Adolescent Sexual Permissiveness." *Adolescence*, Fall 1995.

Swanson, Janice M., Ph.D., R.N. and Chenitz, W. Carole, Ed.D., R.N. "Psychosocial Aspects of Genital Herpes: A Review of the Literature." *Public Health Nursing*, June 1990.

Takahashi, Ayame, M.D. and Franklin, John, M.D. "Alcohol Abuse." *Pediatrics in Review*, February 1996.

Tarter, Ralph E., et al. "Alcohol Use Disorder among Adolescents: Impact of Paternal Alcoholism on Drinking Behavior, Drinking Motivation, and Consequences." *Alcoholism: Clinical and Experimental Research*, February 1997.

Tubman, Jonathan, G., et al. "The Onset and Cross-Temporal Patterning of Sexual Intercourse in Middle Adolescence: Prospective Relations with Behavioral and Emotional Problems." *Child Development*, 1996.

"Update: Trends in AIDS Diagnosis and Reporting Under the Expanded Surveillance Definition for Adolescents and Adults— United States, 1993." *Journal of the American Medical Association*, December 21, 1994.

"Update: Trends in AIDS Incidence, Deaths, and Prevalence—United States, 1996." *Journal of the American Medical Association*, March 19, 1997.

Weinbender, Miriam L. and Rossignol, Annette M. "Lifestyle and Risk of Premature Sexual Activity in a High School Population of Seventh-Day Adventists: Valuegenesis 1989." *Adolescence*, Summer 1996.

White, Sharon D. and DeBlassie, Richard R. "Adolescent Sexual Behavior." *Adolescence*, vol. 27 No. 105, Spring 1992.

Yang, M. "Adolescent Sexuality and Its Problems." *Annals Academy of Medicine*, September 1995.

About the Author

Meg Meeker speaks serves on the National Advisory Board for the Medical Institute and speaks nationally on teen health issues. She has written numerous articles for *Physician* magazine and other parenting periodicals. She practices pediatric and adolescent medicine with her husband, Walter. They have four children, including two teenagers. This is her first book.

ORDER INFORMATION

To order additional copies of *Restoring the Teenage Soul* send a check or money order for $14.95 plus $2.50 for shipping and handling per book to:

McKinley-Mann
940 Pine Ridge Drive
Traverse City, MI 49686

Or call toll-free: **1-877-800-7567**

Quantity discounts are available.

Please send _____ book(s).

Name:_____

Address: _____

_____

City: _____

State: _____ Zip: _____

Telephone:_____

Send check or money order (payable to *McKinley-Mann*) plus above information to:

McKinley-Mann
940 Pine Ridge Drive
Traverse City, MI 49686
1-877-800-7567